PRAYING IN TONGUES IS NORMAL

TERESA VERDECCHIO

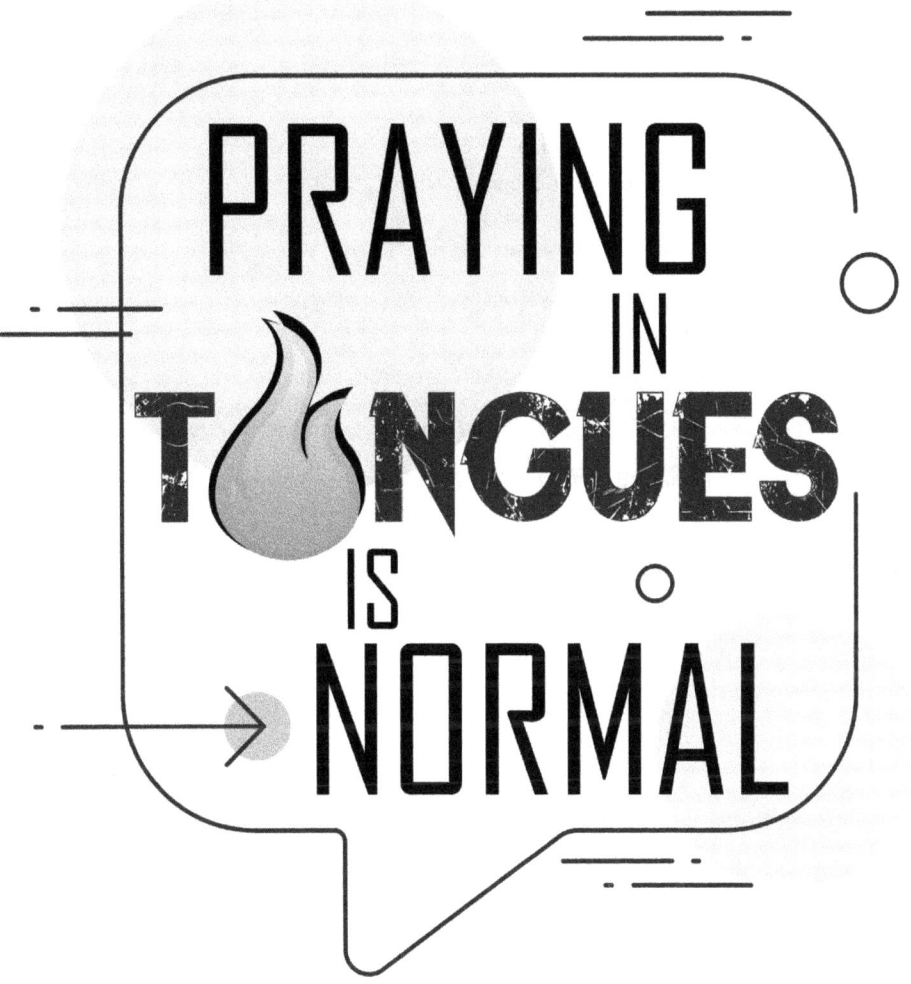

PRAYING IN TONGUES IS NORMAL

Encouraging Spirit-Filled Believers to be Unapologetic About the Gift of Speaking in Tongues

PRAYING IN TONGUES IS NORMAL
© 2022 Teresa Verdecchio.

All rights reserved. No part of this publication may be reproduced, distributed, or transmitted in any form or by any means, including photocopying, recording, or other electronic or mechanical methods, without the prior written permission of the publisher, except in the case of brief quotations embodied in critical reviews and certain other noncommercial uses permitted by copyright law. For permission requests, please contact the author.

    Published by Teresa Verdecchio | Downington, PA
    ISBN (Paperback): 978-1-7352777-3-8
    ISBN (Hardback): 978-1-7352777-4-5
    ISBN (Kindle): 978-1-7352777-5-2
    Library of Congress Control Number (LCCN): 2022901442
    Printed in the United States of America
    Prepared for Publication: www.wendykwalters.com

Scripture quotations marked KJV are taken from the King James Version of the Bible and are in the public domain.

Scripture quotations marked AMP and AMPC are taken from The Amplified Bible® and The Amplified Bible Classic Edition® respectively, Copyright © 1954, 1958, 1962, 1964, 1965, 1987, 2015 by The Lockman Foundation. Used by permission. (www.Lockman.org)

Scripture quotations marked ESV are taken from The Holy Bible, English Standard Version®, copyright © 2001 by Crossway, a publishing ministry of Good News Publishers. Used by permission. All rights reserved.

Scripture quotations marked GW are taken from GOD'S WORD® copyright © 1995, 2003, 2013, 2014, 2019, 2020 by God's Word to the Nations Mission Society. All rights reserved.

Sripture quotations marked J.B. PHILLIPS are taken from The New Testament in Modern English by J.B Phillips copyright © 1960, 1972 J. B. Phillips. Administered by The Archbishops' Council of the Church of England. Used by Permission.

Scripture quotations marked NASB are taken from the New American Standard Bible®, Copyright © 1960, 1962, 1963, 1968, 1971, 1972, 1973, 1975, 1977, 1995 by The Lockman Foundation. Used by permission. (www.Lockman.org)

Scripture quotations marked NIV are taken from THE HOLY BIBLE, NEW INTERNATIONAL VERSION®, Copyright © 1973, 1978, 1984, 2011 by Biblica, Inc.® Used by permission. All rights reserved worldwide.

Scripture quotations marked NKJV are taken from the New King James Version®. Copyright © 1982 by Thomas Nelson. Used by permission. All rights reserved.

Scripture quotations marked NLT are taken from The Holy Bible, New Living Translation, copyright ©1996, 2004, 2007, 2013 by Tyndale House Foundation. Used by permission of Tyndale House Publishers, Inc., Carol Stream, Illinois 60188. All rights reserved.

Scripture quotations marked as TPT are taken from The Passion Translation®. Copyright © 2017 by Passion & Fire Ministries, Inc. Used by permission. All rights reserved. thePassionTranslation.com

To contact the author: www.teresaverdecchio.com

DEDICATION

This book is dedicated to Holy Spirit, my dearest and closest friend. I am humbled that You would pick me to write about You when I know so little. I am taken with You.

ACKNOWLEDGMENTS

The amount of gratitude I feel for my husband is immeasurable. He patiently endured a multitude of random interruptions in our conversations while I captured thoughts for my book. Thank you for always cheering me on and being my biggest fan. You've been with me every step of the way, in every adventure. Our story keeps getting better with every page we turn and I am still so in love with you.

The first time I remember hearing the sound of prayer was through my momma. It grabbed my attention as a little girl and stayed with me. I can never say enough how especially thankful I am to have a praying mother. Thank you, Brenda Peters.

A heartfelt thank you to my NDCC church family for all of your prayers for this project. I am so deeply grateful for you.

A special thank you to Mimi Cirio for your help with the edits. You are an excellent woman and Jesus is fond of you.

I appreciate my leaders who believe in me, cover me, pray for me, and encourage me every step of the way. Thank you Apostle Joe and Pastor Rena Perozich for your encouragement and belief in this book.

Special thanks to my author coach and friend, Wendy Walters, for taking the ideas in my head and helping me turn them into a book. This has been internally challenging and richly rewarding. Thank you for not letting me quit the many times I wanted to. This is a much better book because of you.

PRAISE FOR PRAYING IN TONGUES IS NORMAL

Praying in Tongues is Normal is a thorough, practical, and excellent deep dive into a type of prayer that will change your life forever. Study it, pray like you haven't before, and you will be able to reach your goal of praying for one hour. I highly recommend and endorse Pastor Teresa and her book for readers at all levels of prayer experience. Go ahead and create your new prayer normal!

—MARYALICE ISLEIB
Speaker, Author, Coach | MeetMaryAlice.com

What a joy it is to endorse this book! It is personal, practical, and powerful. It is prophetic—a right now, need-to-read book—not only for the generation arising but the present as well for it provokes curiosity, answers questions, and is accurate in its teachings and applications. It challenges the reader's present mode of existence and results in the realization that the title is accurate: *Praying in Tongues is Normal.* Thank you Pastor Teresa Verdecchio. I truly believe that many will read and be transformed now and in the times to come before Jesus' returns!

—DR. REBECCA POLIS
Vice President, Revival Fellowship International | dr.rebecca@rfiusa.org

There is a grave practice in many modern church settings where everyone wants to feel safe and comfortable all the time. Sadly, the results often eliminate the power of the Holy Spirit to change lives in our midst. Teresa Verdechio has done a marvelous job in this book, *Praying in Tongues is Normal* to shed needed light on this reality. She traces her personal experience with the gift of tongues and then releases a powerful challenge for all of us to speak in tongues often, as well as to allow the Holy Spirit to have His way among the body of Christ. Be prepared to be convicted, encouraged, and challenged by this wonderful book!

—KEITH COLLINS
Founder of Generation Impact Ministries | keith–collins.org
Founder of Impact Global Fellowship | impactgf.org
Host of "Maintain the Flame" Podcast | Charisma Podcast Network | iTunes

In the quick fix society in which we live, it is often forgotten that revelation is progressive (Romans 16:24-25). What you are holding in your hand is more than a book about tongues, it is a journey Pastor Teresa Verdecchio is vulnerably taking readers through—one she first went through herself. It will not just give information, but if the reader will allow, it will bring a transformation. Destined to become a classic for generations to come, *Praying in Tongues is Normal,* is a tool for pastors, evangelists, layman and all who desire to make disciples, not just converts. As Thomas Paine says, "... a long habit of thinking a thing wrong, gives it a superficial appearance of being right, and raises at first a formidable outcry in defense of custom. But, tumult soon subsides. Time makes more converts than reason." Even if you are opposed to tongues, Teresa will convince you otherwise with her easy to read and comprehend language of love she learned from her best friend, the Holy Spirit.

—RENA PEROZICH
Prophet, Pastor, Author, Certified Life, Business, and Ministry Coach
www.renaperozich.com | www.mfcministries.net | www.restorationchurchintl.org

There is revelation that comes when knowledge is applied. The words spoken by doers carry much weight. It is evident that Pastor Teresa has used these principles and they can be applied to create a life of victory.

—JOE PEROZICH
Apostle, Founder, CEO of MFC Ministries, Inc.
www.hoperadio.net | www.mfcministries.net | www.restorationchurchintl.org

I never trust a leader without a limp. I don't follow plastic saints with perfect images. Teresa Verdecchio knows she has feet of clay, and loves God so much that she isn't afraid to live the walk of sanctification in front of us in living color. I grew up with the baptism of the Holy Spirit as a relevant, present part of my life, and *Praying in Tongues is Normal* STILL challenged me to explore the gift from a new light and adventure "further up and further in" with the Holy Spirit. Read it with an open mind and you'll find your curiosity piqued to pray in a new way.

—WENDY K. WALTERS
Speaker, Author, Editor, Adviser | wendykwalters.com

CONTENTS

INTRODUCTION — 1

CHAPTER ONE — 3
A TORMENTED WOMAN

CHAPTER TWO — 11
DESTINY INTERCEPTED

CHAPTER THREE — 17
G.I. JANE

CHAPTER FOUR — 25
MY DEAREST AND CLOSEST FRIEND

CHAPTER FIVE — 41
SEVEN ATTRIBUTES OF THE HOLY SPIRIT

CHAPTER SIX — 59
BREAKING POINT

CHAPTER SEVEN — 73
SURVIVING THE PURGE

CHAPTER EIGHT — 89
THE CALL TO THE NORTHEAST

CHAPTER NINE — 105
BE FILLED

CHAPTER TEN — 117
THE PLACE CALLED "DONE"

CHAPTER ELEVEN 127
CLUB P.I.T.

APPENDIX 153
DIVERSITY OF TONGUES

ABOUT THE AUTHOR 169

INTRODUCTION

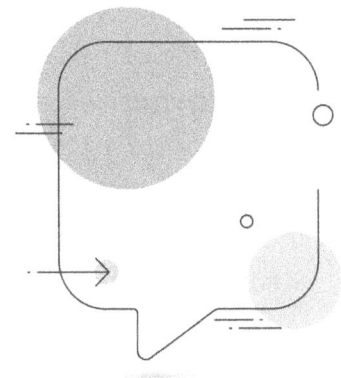

"Leave it to Almighty God to come up with the gift of tongues—a language spoken but not understood ... it takes unwavering faith in Scripture to practice praying in tongues ..."

—BOB ENGLEHARDT

Praying in Tongues is Normal is my attempt at throwing ink at the devil. I have found that praying in tongues has kept the enemy out of the equation. It has reversed his destructive plans for my life as the Holy Spirit started praying through me, for me, and in me.

Far too many years of my life were spent in frustration. When I began to learn the power of being full of the Holy Spirit and under His influence, I began to draw on Him for comfort, peace, and guidance. I share with transparency the process of a transformed life when I began to, on purpose, pray in the Holy Ghost. **Praying in the Spirit for edification results in transformation.**

I hope to encourage Spirit-filled believers to be unapologetic and intentional about the gift of speaking in tongues. I believe it is time that we stop cowering in the corners embarrassed and stop dismissing the Holy Spirit to a side room because we cannot explain Him or how He moves. He is not weird. He is the third person of the Godhead. He has been entrusted to be our Guide, helping us maneuver through the trials and tribulations of this life, effectively leading us to our appointed destination.

We aren't going to understand or even agree about some things, but we can all agree that we need a move of Holy Ghost power and demonstration. We need an awakening. A revival. A powerful encounter with Jesus Christ in our lives, families, neighborhoods, and nation. How will we ever have a move of the Holy Spirit if we think we can contain and market Him? We won't. In fact, He wants to mark us and distinctly set us apart for a God-glorifying work. The Holy Spirit has been sent to assist us. He is our Helper.

The pages of this book will focus on the benefit of praying in tongues, and I will share its impact on my personal life. Praying in tongues is not fictional—*Praying in Tongues is Normal!* This is my message to the Body of Christ in this book. The gift of tongues did not cease with the apostles, nor is it only for a select few; rather, speaking in tongues is a normal and biblical tool in the plan of God to save, heal, deliver, and release each believer into destiny.

I offer my story of how praying in the Spirit altered my world, moving me closer to the perfect will of God. It is my hope that you will be inspired as you take a journey with me inside these pages to perhaps ponder what your life could look like if you just released the Holy Spirit to pray through you. If you already practice praying in tongues, may you be inspired to stir the gift at a greater level.

CHAPTER ONE

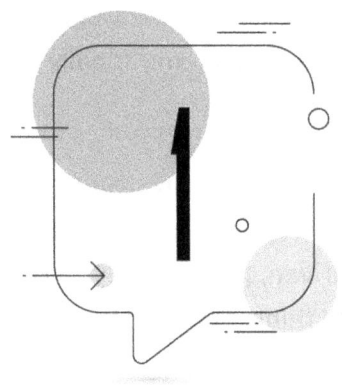

A TORMENTED WOMAN

"Hope itself is like a star—not to be seen in the sunshine of prosperity, and only to be discovered in the night of adversity."

—C.H. SPURGEON

What's wrong with me? Will I ever measure up? Will I ever just get out of my own way? I'm not even sure it is possible for me to become all God says I can be ...

I was miserable. My mind was trapped in a hopeless tangle of tormented beliefs. Condemnation. Judgment. Failure. Accusation. These thoughts bombarded me without reprieve—I was under siege, like a once-beautiful city now charred and unrecognizable after constant enemy attack. A single harmless thought would unleash, pulling me in every direction until my mind was fragmented and I was in anguish. Tired and frustrated, I had grown weary from battling against depression and emotionally drained from wrestling with oppression.

By day, no one had a clue about my struggle. I was high-functioning. I masked my depression with manic activity, and everyone knew my reputation as a driven, productive young woman. The thought of what people would think if my performance plummeted created intense anxiety. I feared exposure. So, responsibility became my drug of choice. Being a performance-oriented wife and mother forced me to push back the darkness just enough to engage each day. At night, however, the demons roared. I had no peace. I was the kind of exhausted that sleep does not answer, which was a good thing because I never slept.

Perpetual insomnia left me so sleep-deprived that I was perpetually irritable, fighting brain fog, and filled with anxiety that I am astounded the slimy voice of suicide never won. I heard it often, offering an end to the anguish, wrapping depression around me like a cozy, warm blanket. Suicide promised comfort in the abyss of escape. But each time I was seriously tempted, another Voice always called to me—that Voice spoke my name and breathed hope into my weary soul.

I needed a breakthrough ... or I was going to break.

I loved God for as long as I can remember. My earliest childhood memories all have the knowledge and acceptance of God woven through them. I received prophecies as a child and throughout my twenties, but an honest look at my life revealed that not much looked like the declared promises I had received from

God's servants. I was terribly oppressed, and nothing I attempted seemed to set me free. Occasionally, I had moments of reprieve, only to be imprisoned again by the cruel thought taskmaster and the ferocious feelings that accompanied him.

There was no escape.

My thoughts raced in twenty different directions, and everything on the inside was chaotic. No matter how much effort I exerted, I felt doomed to failure. Nothing worked. I was walking potential, but I became a frustrated and emotionally distraught mess.

I listened to great sermons on the promises of God, but somehow I missed the practical application. I wanted someone to show me how to take the positional truths that I knew were accurate because of all Jesus did to make His God my God and His Father my Father. But the question still begged to be asked ... *what am I missing? Why isn't this working in my life? How do I take these spiritual truths and get them to work practically in my life?*

As a believer, I knew I had eternal life, but I wasn't living in eternity; I was living in the here and now. What good does knowing my eternal destination do me if my temporal existence is filled with torment? Jesus promised, "I have come to give you life and that more abundantly" (John 10:10, ESV). I could quote this—preach on it—but I needed to experience this abundant life as my reality! Where was that at? ... Where was this "abundant life"?

I knew the problem was not with God; it lay with my skewed perception of God. Yet, the problem remained. I looked fine on the outside, but inside I was suffocating. I would hear things like, "think your way to victory," or "confess the Word of God," and though these were all correct principles, my attempts always fell short. Whatever I tried, whatever I memorized, confessed, or declared, soon degenerated their way back into destructive thinking patterns. It would cramp my brain! I'd read the Bible over and over. I could quote multitudes of scriptures I had memorized and written deep in my heart, but it brought no lasting change to my life. Rather it was a constant reminder of how even God's promises eluded me.

Instead of offering life, hope, and encouragement, the devil used God's Word against me to condemn me. I fell short. Always. I was evil. I was depraved. I was sick in my sin. I was unclean. My thought patterns created systems of failure deeply ingrained in my brain, and I felt hopeless for any lasting change. I accepted that God would do His part faithfully. I could not accept, however, that God already knew and had factored in my failure as part of His covenant. Positionally, I knew I was righteous because Jesus is righteousness, and I was positioned in Him. Practically, however, I knew I was filthy rags. Unless and until I could find the discipline, grit, fortitude … whatever … to never put the filthy grave clothes back on voluntarily, then I was not acceptable to God—not worthy of His sacrifice. I knew I couldn't earn my salvation; it was a gift from God. Still, I couldn't reconcile that my tormented thoughts and actions did not mount evidence against the condition of my soul that could somehow "un-earn" my salvation. After all, faith without works is dead, isn't it?

> **TWISTED TRUTH IS MORE DANGEROUS THAN AN OUTRIGHT LIE**

Twisted truth is more dangerous than an outright lie.

My attempts to obey biblical principles such as "cast down every thought and imagination" (2 Corinthians 10:5) were valiant.

However, the thoughts were so relentless that I grew exhausted. I wanted to quit, yet something inside would not allow me to. I knew that some way, somehow, there had to be hope even though mentally and emotionally, I felt like I was shattered into millions of pieces. I was afraid to hope. Every time I had allowed myself the luxury of hope, the bottom would fall out again, and I was left devastated. I was desperate for answers, for understanding. *Where was the peace so often promised in the Gospel? Why didn't I work on the inside?*

I was damaged goods. Something was obviously wrong with me.

I managed to keep up appearances through performance and vigorous religious activity, a trait I learned in childhood. No matter what was happening, I functioned, but that was quickly unraveling. All the things I had refused to deal with—the haunting memories, buried burdens, the secrets and shame from the abuse I suffered and the sins I partook of—were taking their toll. The last thing I wanted to do was pillage through the burdened backpack I had been carrying. Condemnation was my constant companion. I had no idea that in this backslidden condition, battle-weary and in a frighteningly familiar place of wanting to bolt, God was about to run after me!

God was about to switch up the Companion I was backpacking through life with.

I do not exaggerate the darkness I lived in. I give it no glory. I speak with candor and make no attempt to gloss over my story because I want to create a place of safety where others can risk stepping into their vulnerable place and finding real and lasting hope. I honestly wanted just to be erased from life. I was miserable, yet I seemingly had no reason for such intense emotions and thoughts. I had a wonderful husband who had been nothing but patient and kind to me even though he didn't understand my battles. I was blessed with a beautiful daughter who was full of joy and laughter and an amazing little boy full of adventure. Life was good ... even this caused me misery because I felt I didn't deserve any of it!

God knew what He was doing when He gave me those two kids. They were the reason I resisted the temptation of suicide. I didn't dismiss it, but I kept it on the back burner. One day when I was in the depths of despair and thinking of checking out for good, my daughter suddenly reached up and touched my hand and said, "Momma, I love you. You're special!" Her words snapped me out of that demonic, seducing lie to take my life! Where would I be without my kids? God only knows. If it had not been for His grace ...

My desperation grew. Up and down like a yo-yo. On fire, then under fire. I loved God but didn't feel like I could live for Him because I just couldn't get it together. My life didn't work, though it appeared I had all the raw material to have a great life. How was God going to unwrap me from what I got wrapped up in?

My internal struggles undoubtedly stemmed from my earliest years when the concrete was being formed on the inside. In my book, *Crushing Condemnation,* I share how my childhood was wrought with the cruel weapons of abuse—the kind of abuse that soils the soul deeply. When a child is violated, though they survive the experiences, they're left with the residuals of confusion, insecurity, and shame, just to name a few. Children do not believe something bad happened to them; they believe, "I am bad."

You don't "age out" of the emotional baggage from childhood. Unless you learn how to empty it and be made whole, you carry it with you through life. Unwilling to claim victim status, I became a "keep it moving" kind of person. I didn't deal with anything; I stuffed it down deep and hid it from everyone. But my emotions were catching up to me, and I found myself in a vicious cycle—either in a dungeon of depression or a volcanic explosion of anger and rage. Something had to give. I was desperate.

But deliverance is for the desperate.

INTERNAL STRUGGLES CAN MAKE YOU FEEL DESPERATE—BUT DELIVERANCE IS FOR THE DESPERATE.

CHAPTER TWO

DESTINY INTERCEPTED

"Divine life is full of divine appointment and equipping, and you cannot be filled with the power of God without a manifestation. It is my prayer that we would understand that to be filled with the Holy Spirit is to be filled with manifestation, the glory of the Lord being in the midst of us, manifesting His divine power."

—SMITH WIGGLESWORTH

One day changed my life. God sent a prophet—a divine appointment—a woman with a message and a mission. It was a day I'll never forget. I was at a women's conference in the mountains of beautiful Colorado. I had gone reluctantly after being nagged until I yielded to the person blessing me. My husband had also encouraged me to go. Looking back, I'm sure it was to get relief from his miserable, angry, brooding wife. I know he was hoping God would intervene. Dave loved me unconditionally, but if something didn't happen, our marriage was over. We both knew it.

I attended the conference, but I hated it. I rolled my eyes the whole time. Due to my warped self-image, each session was a reminder of the failure, mistakes, and seemingly lost promises that haunted me every day. Every break or free moment found me alone, shooting hoops and walking in the beautiful mountains. I was barely enduring the conference.

Ironically, the guest speaker was someone I had admired since I was a teenager. It was she who had inspired me to be a woman of God when I saw her preaching in a park on a Saturday afternoon during an outreach. I was drawn to her boldness and obvious love for Jesus. Her passion was fire, and it captured me. Yet here I was a little over a decade later. I listened to her, filled with even more zeal and love for Jesus she had gained over the years, but I was dead inside.

I participated through pure muscle memory. I knew how to act, when to sing, when to stand, when to sit. I dutifully took notes and tried my best to make sure I looked like I was engaged. As the conference was winding to its conclusion, I was glad I had survived. I had my exit plan in place. With just one more session to endure, I'd be out of there. I already had my Honda packed and couldn't wait to get off that mountain! They were wrapping up with an altar call when I made my exit. I was outside, in the clear when suddenly I heard my name being shouted.

No! my mind raged. *Keep walking!* I said to myself and quickened my pace.

No good. I heard a whistle. This immediately grabbed my attention, and I froze. Being a girls' basketball coach, I was accustomed to the whistle. It demanded that the game stop and you pay attention to the referee. Like I said, muscle memory. Instinct. Little did I know, God was about to use this servant of His to intercept my life. He was about to enter my life in a dramatic way.

Whipping my head around, I noticed that this woman had run after me. Though I had slipped out before the meeting had ended to avoid talking to anyone, she had actually left the service to follow me when she saw me exit.

"Teresa, what is wrong with you? What happened to you?" she called out as she closed the distance between us.

I stood stunned, not sure how to answer her.

"Do you think I came all the way from Seoul, South Korea, just to come to this women's conference?"

I shrugged my shoulders.

"I didn't," she smiled, "I was in a prayer grotto in Cho's church, and God told me, 'Go back to the States and find Teresa Verdecchio; she's in trouble.' I have been praying for you for six months," she said. She paused and looked at me intently, "Teresa, you need to get right with God. Your heart is backslidden."

I said something cocky.

She wasn't intimidated.

She moved closer and ripped my expensive sunglasses off my face, and demanded I look her in the eyes. "Five years! " she said as she held up all five fingers of her hand right in my face. "Five years from now, I will either hear FROM you or ABOUT you. You'll either have backslidden, split hell wide open, and be a blasphemer of God losing your husband and children, or you will be preaching the Gospel of Jesus Christ! Now you have a choice to make."

Angered, I retorted, "Happy (expletive) 27th birthday to me!" and turned from her to walk away.

She grabbed me by the collar and said, "It can either be the best birthday of your life or the worst! You have a decision to make! I call you to repentance."

She spoke with such earnest authority that my tough exterior began to crack. I stood frozen, and her silence was holy and terrifying.

I broke. Stunned, I felt hot tears run down my face. It had been a while since I dropped my mask, and I began to cry.

"Teresa, go get in your car and repent on the drive down the mountain. Ask Jesus to forgive you," she instructed. Then she told me the most life-changing thing I had heard up to that point. "You must pray one hour a day in tongues. Pray in the Holy Ghost—it is crucial. I don't care if you have to set your alarm clock for one hour a day. But the key to you making it and getting out of this mess is to pray for one hour a day in tongues."

I didn't completely understand what she meant, but something deep in me had an awareness that she had given me a secret to climbing out of the pit.

"I love you," she said, then prayed over me as she hugged me tightly. I melted into her arms, relieved she had called me out.

She didn't know what the outcome of talking with me would be. But she did what God had told her to do, and she administered it in the way I needed to hear it—direct, no room for interpretation, decisive confrontation.

I am delighted to report by the grace of God that exactly five years later, she did indeed hear FROM me, not ABOUT me. Though that servant of God had not heard from me one time since the day of that wild encounter, I am sure she smiled when she received mail of a recording of me preaching the Gospel.

That day I had a meeting with destiny.

God was about to set me on a journey that would align me with the call of heaven. All the days ordained for me were written in His book before one of them came to be (Psalm 139:16).

"How do I discover that book?" I questioned, not knowing that praying in tongues is praying the perfect will of God and the personal plan of God for my life. When I pray in the Holy Spirit, I tap into heaven's plan. God planned every last detail of my life, and He didn't leave me to myself but gave me a way I could have His plan revealed. Anytime I want to work God's perfect plan in my life, if I will just pray in the Holy Ghost, He goes ahead of me and clears the path. He begins to draw everything to me that is needed for my life.

When I pray in tongues, the Holy Spirit goes out ahead of me to bring me whatever I need to fulfill the assignment of God.

> WHEN I PRAY IN TONGUES, THE HOLY SPIRIT GOES OUT AHEAD OF ME TO BRING ME WHATEVER I NEED TO FULFILL THE ASSIGNMENT OF GOD

So, what happened, you might ask? I was curious. My mind was blown that God would speak so specifically to someone about my plight, then send them on a rescue mission from another continent to recover me and give me a key! Well, I would be a fool not to at least try what she said to me, right?

I repented all the way down that mountain, tears flowing unchecked. I went home and did exactly what she had said to do, though I did not fully understand it. I started praying in tongues an hour each day. I had been baptized in the Holy Ghost since I was eight, but like many, I didn't really exercise the gift of tongues. So, I literally set my alarm clock and prayed in tongues for one hour a day.

Most days, I couldn't wait for that alarm clock to go off. But regardless of what was going on in my circumstances or emotions, I would report to the prayer closet daily without fail. I didn't really notice much change at first, and I was irritated and experienced a gamut of thoughts and emotions, but I was also so very curious.

Her showing up when I was so desperate and crying out for intervention had intrigued me. I knew what my life looked like without praying in the Spirit. *What would it look like if I was stubborn enough not to quit?*

With that resolve, I just kept praying in tongues. I had no idea of the transformative journey I was about to embark on with God. I would experience Him in a way I had only dreamt of.

CHAPTER THREE

G.I. JANE

"There is something about believing God that will cause
Him to pass over a million people to get to you."

—SMITH WIGGLESWORTH

At the end of six months of praying in tongues, I suddenly heard God speak to me—like *REALLY* speak to me on the inside. I nearly froze. It had been a very long time since I heard Him speak like this. Although I had been praying faithfully, I had not heard much of His voice outside of reading the Word. I was listening to a message, and in the middle of it, God told me to go to another city and speak to this particular woman. I thought, *Do you mean this woman I am listening to preaching?*

It shook me so much that I ignored it. But the voice kept getting louder and louder. I kept disregarding it and kept praying in tongues. Finally, I was so uncomfortable ignoring it, and my insomnia was so severe that if "that Voice" had told me to go talk to a cow, I would have, just for the hope of finding relief!

I did some research and located the woman's ministry office. I was so determined I would obey what I heard that after tracking her down, I walked into the office and asked if I could see her. The receptionist looked at me dumbfounded. "Do you have an appointment?" she asked.

"No," I answered, "I don't have an appointment, but I really need to see her."

Even I knew I sounded like a crazy stalker and was not surprised when the receptionist said, "I'm afraid she's not in right now."

"That's okay. I'll wait outside. I must see her," and I went out to the parking lot.

I waited for over an hour, growing impatient. The restlessness got to me, so I went to get my Jeep washed and grab a bite to eat. *Surely this woman would be back in the office by now*, I thought. I went back inside and inquired again.

"I'm so sorry," she shook her head, "she is still not available. Would you like to leave a message for her?"

"No," I replied, "I will wait!" The Holy Spirit had told me to go see this woman, and I was determined to do just that. I had already arranged for my kids to be picked up from school and be taken care of. I was fully prepared to do a stakeout if that is what it took. There was a reason God was leading me to talk to a complete stranger.

Several hours went by. I did not know that I was waiting for another appointment with destiny or how worth the wait would prove to be. God had another encounter planned for me. I ran another errand to fuel up and went back to the parking lot.

For the third time, I went to ask the kind woman at the desk if I could speak with the minister, but before I could ask, I heard a voice down the hall say, "I heard you want to speak with me."

"Yes!" I said, "Thank you!"

The woman introduced herself and invited me into her office.

I will respectfully refer to this woman as G.I. Jane. She was gracious enough to meet with a total stranger. I would come to learn that she was also tough enough to take on the likes of me, and God used her to train and mentor me.

Once in her office, I assumed she would think I was nuts when I told her how God was having me pray in tongues an hour a day and that, as a result of doing so, God had told me specifically to seek her out. "Initially, I resisted," I told her, "it felt crazy, but I finally decided I would rather be thought a fool than disobey the first thing I had heard Him say."

As I told my story, she grinned. She seemed to understand me. At times her eyes filled with tears of compassion, which baffled me. She patiently waited as I spilled it all out. I had nothing to lose. This woman was a total stranger whom I thought I would never see again, so I threw all caution to the wind and spilled it all—the deep, dark, tormenting desires that would wreck my life along with such brokenness that I just wanted to run.

On the one hand, I hoped my life would just be erased, yet on the other, I knew I was created and called by God to preach and do something with Him in the earth. I thought for sure she was going to say, "Lady, you're crazy!" Instead, she said, "That's not your problem at all! Do you want to know what your problem is?"

I looked at her like, *Well ... yeah ... what a question!*

"Your problem," she continued, "is that you're running from the call of God on your life!"

Immediately and instinctively, I ducked! I had run into another prophet!

"Can I pray for you?" she asked.

What was I going to say? "Of course," I agreed and braced myself as she came around her desk and began to pray over me. She prayed strongly in the Spirit and started to go into intercession for me. I had recognized this kind of intense prayer from growing up with a praying mother—one who gave herself to "groaning in the Holy Spirit." On a few occasions when life became too heavy for me, I myself had experienced that kind of prayer. That kind of prayer has a sound you will never forget.

That woman wept and wailed in prayer over me as she prayed in tongues. All I knew was that something broke off of me that day, and it felt like I could breathe again for the first time in a very long time. I was, in that moment, delivered from the demonic bondage of oppression. I cannot describe the peace that flooded my heart, mind, and body. It was supernatural. I slept for a day after that experience.

God had divinely connected me to G.I. Jane. In that appointment with destiny, He had divinely connected me to another of His servants who had the revelation of praying in tongues.

To my surprise, one Sunday morning at church, there was a cassette tape (this was 25 years ago) on my chair. I looked at it and realized that G.I. Jane had given me something to listen to. It was a teaching on the subject of praying in tongues. After listening to one message, I was hooked. I was so hungry for God. I gained some understanding of what praying in the Holy Spirit did for us. I was blessed to eventually meet and come to know this second minister and learn directly from him about praying in tongues. His message on praying in the Spirit was THE message that put it all together for me. The Gospel began to click. It started to make sense. I had stumbled onto a revelatory gift.

Understanding was flooding my mind as hope filled my soul.

Some have asked me over the years why I am so committed to praying in tongues. I am devoted to it and passionate about teaching others about this gift. My simple answer—it changed my life. I had an about-face. Literally, it has changed me from the inside out. God was not intimidated by my mess. He was overjoyed the day I decided to partner up with the Holy Ghost and start allowing Him to pray through me. Anyone that knows me, knows I am ardent about praying in tongues. I honor the teachers God sent me who had the revelation of praying in the Spirit.

I experienced radical change and shifts in my soul as all permanent change happens from the inside out. Once I stopped looking for my circumstances to change, I realized the miracle that was taking place was showing up in my person changing. I settled into the process. As a result, Holy Spirit has toppled lifelong bondages, stubborn strongholds, generational curses, and patterns of failure. Jesus was manifested to destroy the works of the devil. He literally destroyed what was destroying me. All I had to do was show up and let Holy Spirit pray through me. It was a journey I took out of desperation that ended up being the most wonderful adventure as I got to know the third person of the Godhead, the Holy Spirit.

The Bible encourages us:

> "But ye, beloved, building up yourselves on your most holy faith, by praying in the Holy Ghost …"
>
> JUDE 1:20, KJV

As I continued to pray more and more in the Spirit and under the tutelage of G.I. Jane, I started learning so much. Things difficult to understand began to be revealed, especially as I read my Bible. The more I prayed, the more I wanted to pray. Change started to show up. I began to notice destructive emotions and thought patterns of my soul breaking off. I would realize over time they were no longer present. Thoughts toward myself were a litter kinder. I noticed I no longer emotionally and impulsively reacted but made healthier responses. The Holy Spirit was doing the heavy lifting. All I had to do was show up and utter the syllables of this amazing language.

In the book *Walk of the Spirit, Walk of Power,* Dave Roberson states,

> *The Holy Ghost knows God's mind for every dispensation and generation for every moment in conjunction with my call and with revival. He is fully equipped when I spend the night in edification to move me ahead in that plan, understanding all of my problems, my shortcomings, what He has to move out of my way, what He has to do to edify and to build me*

up on my most holy faith. He understands God's plan, His mind for my city, my church and for my individual. He and He alone is the only one alive that can make intercession for me according to the plan of God, that I can know everything will eventually be pulled in and will turn out for my overall good and purpose of God which is revival and getting people saved. He utters syllables of victory. He's the one that really knows what's holding me back. He knows my problem. He knows my call, but He knows in the moment of time God's mind in my role in fulfilling it. He's the earner of my inheritance and nobody has the position He has in my life. The Holy Ghost must express something and get me to pray it. It releases Him to work on impossible things in my life, in my spirit, and where my authority is. Your miracle, your anointing, call, and equipping. The Holy Ghost is ordained to do what no one else in my life can do—step into the patterns of my failures and break their cycle. Not only can He break the patterns of my past, but He can establish God's plan for my future. One of the enemy's greatest weapons is to keep me repeating the past. When the Holy Ghost is directing my future, He has the power to pull me into it and His direction gets stronger and stronger.

I was thrilled as I started to understand the benefit of praying in the Spirit. Every time I prayed, I was partnering with the Holy Spirit in building the house of my life. Anytime we pray in our heavenly prayer language, it edifies and builds us up on our faith, preparing us to fulfill our God-given destinies.

"He who speaks in a tongue edifies himself ..."

1 CORINTHIANS 14:4A, NKJV

Websters 1828 Dictionary defines **edify** as "building up in Christian knowledge; instructing; improving the mind." The *New Living Translation* says "is strengthened personally," *God's Word* translation says, "helps himself grow," and the *Christian Standard Bible* says "builds himself up."

This is exactly what was taking place in my life, and I was beyond excited!

While I prayed, Holy Spirit was busy laying a foundation complete with pillars, beams, columns, and constructing rooms for me to house His anointing. The Holy Spirit teaches kingdom of God principles—the law of the Spirit that governs the kingdom—and those principles began to govern my life.

When you pray in the Spirit, mysteries are unlocked. Nobody knows the plan and counsel of God for your life other than God. When we pray in tongues, we are turning the Holy Spirit loose to work that plan. I see Him as a Project Manager. He works all things according to our good because He knows the mind of the Spirit and the counsel of God for you.

> WHEN YOU PRAY IN THE SPIRIT, MYSTERIES ARE UNLOCKED

Let me encourage you to do this: **pray in tongues because it builds up your inner man.** What have you got to lose?

CHAPTER FOUR

MY DEAREST AND CLOSEST FRIEND

"You'll never feel alone when you have a friendship with the Holy Spirit."

—ROBERT MORRIS

Who is the Holy Spirit? The Holy Spirit is God. The Trinity is made up of God the Father, God the Son, and God the Holy Spirit. God is three distinct parts, yet one. Each Person of the Trinity operates individually, yet all together in perfect unity. The Holy Spirit is every bit God just as the Father and Jesus are God. He is not a lesser part of the Trinity. His role is not inferior to that of Jesus. He is not vague. He is not weaker. He is God, the Holy

Spirit. He is omniscient, all-knowing. He perfectly knows all things, past, present, and future. He is omnipotent. He is all-powerful and sovereign, and no one can thwart His purpose. He is also omnipresent. He is simultaneously everywhere all of the time.

Holy Spirit is a person. He has a personality, a mind, will, and emotions. He is sensitive and can be grieved. We must see Him as He truly is. The third person of the Trinity is not lesser somehow because of being third; that was only the order in which He was introduced to us. Let us look at His entrance in the New Testament.

The moment we believed, we received the Holy Spirit with promise (Ephesians 1:13). Unlike the early believers, we are not waiting on the Holy Spirit; we have Him right now.

When Holy Spirit takes up residence on the inside, we have the privilege of being in relationship with Jesus and Father, as well as having eternal life. Salvation would have been enough for us, but that wasn't enough for God; He wanted to give us a part of Himself, a little bit of heaven on earth. He desired to live in us through the Person of the Holy Spirit, to walk and talk with us in the here and now. He wasn't going to wait until we were in heaven. He came to assist us, to be our traveling companion.

We need to be filled with God's Spirit as we yield to His conviction in our lives through obedience. What is happening in us shows up on the outside. As we become sanctified, we start acting, thinking, and behaving more like Jesus.

When you were saved, all of God's Spirit was present in you. The Holy Spirit lives in you, and now all of His fruit is available to you. When you are at the end of your own natural ability, He takes you beyond. For example, the Holy Spirit helps you live beyond yourself when facing a problem. He gives you patience for that difficult person you cannot handle one moment longer. He gives supernatural self-control, so you have discipline in areas where you know that left to your natural desires and propensities, you would not have control in that area of weakness. Because the Holy Spirit lives in you, you can live beyond your own limited capacity. The Holy Spirit gives us fruit to bless our lives with the ability to live beyond ourselves (Galatians 5:22-23). We also received His gifts (1 Corinthians 12), so we can edify and build one another up.

Ask God to anoint what you do. Ask Him to put fire on what you do. If that is speaking or writing, playing music, administering medicine, or leading your family or a business, ask for His presence to be upon you. He is already **in** you. You want Him to be **on** you—on what you are doing. When you speak to someone, you want the presence of God covering your words because the Holy Spirit is upon you. Yes, perfect your craft, but in the end, what you are looking for is not talent but the gift of the Holy Spirit anointing you as only He can.

I want to be like Simeon, who didn't just have the Spirit *in* him, but the Holy Ghost was ***upon*** him (Luke 2:25). This scripture tells us there is a difference between "in" and "on." I want to live a life that invites the presence of God's Spirit on my life. God is **in** me, but I want Him **upon** me. I desire the kind of life that calls and draws the favor, grace, and anointing of God. I want the evidence of Him on my life. I want the Holy Spirit to hover over me. When I do something, I don't want people to say, "Teresa was there," I want them to say, "the Spirit of God was there." I desire to live in yielded surrender. I want His presence on my life.

I want to be marked by the Spirit of God. I know what it is to be marred; I want to be marked. I want to be marked by the Spirit and presence of God; to be set apart, a distinction, with fire in my belly burning for His holiness; and to carry something unusual and intangible on my life, so that others see something about me that they cannot put their finger on—the favor of God.

The favor of God opens doors. It sets you in positions where you don't belong, qualifying you when you don't have the degree. When the favor of God places you somewhere, and God's Spirit is on your life, you don't have to market or promote yourself because God has marked you.

WHAT ATTRACTS THE PRESENCE OF GOD TO REST ON OUR LIFE?

The one thing that most invites the presence of God on our lives is holiness. Holiness. Plain ole' holiness. Paul instructs us to walk in a manner worthy to which we are called (Ephesians 4:1). We must not live in a way that is incongruent with the Word. We must want to walk holy before our God. Lord, help us to be more interested in receiving the applause of heaven than that of man. We will give an account for all we've done. When we do that, we should be looking to hear, "Well done!" We don't want to miss God, so we want our ears open when He is trying to speak to us. If we want His Spirit on our lives, we must decide to live holy.

> "... we must let go of every wound that has pierced us and the sin we so easily fall into. Then we will be able to run life's marathon race with passion and determination, for the path has been already marked out before us."
>
> HEBREWS 12:1 TPT

I encourage you to lay aside anything that entangles you and keeps you from running the race that is set before you. Every weight. Every wound. Every relationship. Every sin—*anything* that hinders you from walking holy—any addiction, habit, or lifestyle choice that is keeping you from being free and walking in victory in Jesus' name. Let it go by the power of the Holy Spirit so He can rest upon your life.

You want God's presence upon you, marking you and making a distinction from those around you. This happens only when you walk in a manner worthy of this calling. The Holy Spirit invites you into this kind of walk, saying, "Be ye holy."

Holiness is not perfection. It is not a list of rules to keep, boxes to check, or duties to perform. Holiness is a call to the Holy Spirit living in you who empowers you to live in a way that you will not yield to all the desires of your flesh. Holiness means you choose a lifestyle, an attitude, and actions that please God, and you set aside—consciously walk away from—any lifestyle, attitude, or action that you know is displeasing to God. Walk away from everything that keeps you from God's presence which marks you with His purpose and power. The Holy Spirit wants you holy so you can see God, hear His voice, and have an encounter with Him.

> WALK AWAY FROM EVERYTHING THAT KEEPS YOU FROM GOD'S PRESENCE WHICH MARKS YOU WITH HIS PURPOSE AND POWER

Accept the challenge to come up higher. Refuse any shame or condemnation when you have fallen or lived below the call. Simply repent and be restored. By grace, we wear the righteousness of Christ because our best efforts are but filthy rags (Isaiah 64:6). We can *only* live holy because He dwells inside us, and He is holy. Purpose in your heart to get right before the Lord and honor Him and your actions and attitudes.

Our relationship with Holy Spirit is just that—a relationship. Life can get busy, subtly crowding out the connection with Him if we don't guard it. How humbling it was that He came after me. How grateful I am that I responded to Him. He met me. He touched that place that only He can touch. I am forever changed in His presence. I love the Holy Spirit. He is my dearest and closest friend. He knows my full backstory. He knows my history. He is praying me out of everything I was and into everything I am to be. He can be trusted. He makes all things new.

WHO IS THE HOLY SPIRIT?

In Acts 2, the Bible records the Holy Ghost arriving on the scene with a demonstration of power. I have been to the Upper Room in Jerusalem, so I have quite the visual when reading this passage of scripture. The Holy Ghost came to baptize them with fire. It is altogether God's business how He decides to do things, and this was how He chose to make His entrance. He filled the early believers with His Spirit, and they began to speak in other tongues. It caused quite a ruckus then, and it still causes one now.

The Holy Spirit came to empower us, fill us, teach us, lead and guide us. He is the ultimate Helper. He came with purpose. He is strength. He is power. He came onto the scene in a dramatic way. When you believe in Jesus, the Holy Spirit takes up residence in your heart. We see the strength, demonstration, and power of the Holy Ghost on the Day of Pentecost, but there is also another side to the Holy Spirit. Yes, He comes as fire, but He is also gentle as a dove. There is a comforting, nurturing side to the Holy Spirit. If I may say it this way, it is like the mother side of the heart of Father God. God is a complete being, so it only makes sense that He contains the fullness of all paternal and maternal gifts within the Trinity.

> "For Yahweh says, 'I will extend to her prosperity like a river and the wealth of gentiles like a flooding river. You will nurse from her breast, be cradled in her arms, and delightfully bounced on her knees.'"
>
> ISAIAH 66:12, TPT

In the Amplified Classic, it reads this way:

> "For thus says the Lord: 'Behold, I will extend peace to her (Jerusalem) like a river, and the glory of the nations like an overflowing stream; then you will be nursed, you will be carried on her hip and trotted [lovingly bounced up and down] on *her* [God's maternal] knees.'"

This verse reveals God's gentle, mothering side. The Holy Spirit is tender. He knows how to handle the broken without breaking them even further. He is always present. He sees us, the real us without the façade, and He understands us completely and compassionately. He knew us before we were broken. He also sees the totally healed version—the future perfect tense of us throughout eternity—when all things are made new. Nothing horrifies Him about our journey, not even the messy middle. The Holy Spirit sees the end from the beginning and all the points in between. He has been entrusted with us.

THE HOLY SPIRIT KNOWS HOW TO HANDLE THE BROKEN WITHOUT BREAKING THEM FURTHER

See His heart and ministry in this scripture:

> "A broken reed He will not break [off] and a dimly burning wick He will not extinguish [He will not harm those who are weak and suffering]; He will faithfully bring forth justice."
>
> ISAIAH 42:3, AMP

Acts 2 tells us they all spoke in tongues. When the Holy Spirit comes, there is an overflowing experience of speaking in tongues. Tongues—*glossolalia*—is a heavenly language. Holy Spirit baptizes us with fire. Fire represents a purifying agent. Fire to our life brings the dross of our soul to the surface. His fire burns up the defeating debris and purifies us. There is both an indwelling and an infilling of the Spirit. When we are born again, there is an indwelling—He comes to live (dwell) in our heart. When He baptizes us in the Holy Ghost with the evidence of speaking in tongues, there is an infilling—He pours His power, revelation, and goodness into our spirit. The Holy Spirit wants to dwell in each of us in a greater capacity. It was His idea to do it this way.

We see several examples in the book of Acts. Here's one:

> "While Peter was speaking, the Holy Spirit cascaded over all those listening to his message. The Jewish brothers who had accompanied Peter were astounded that the gift of the Holy Spirit was poured out on people who weren't Jews, for they heard them speaking in supernaturally given languages and passionately praising God."
>
> ACTS 10:44-46, TPT

The gift of the Holy Spirit was poured out on the Gentiles, and witnesses heard them speak in tongues. Holy Spirit is expressive. He does not want us to be ashamed of Him, dismissing Him to a side room and telling Him we don't want Him to mess up our nice church services, but He can come out when the visitors leave. Remember, He is a person with feelings. To be ashamed of Him and how He chooses to manifest Himself to and through us or in the church would grieve Him.

Receiving the baptism of the Holy Spirit and speaking in tongues is not about any specific denomination. Walking in the Spirit does not make you weird. He is not legalistic or religious. He is not boring but adventurous. The Holy Spirit is not weird. People are weird, and I do not want to limit what I know or experience about God through a person, not when I have an invitation to know and experience Him for myself.

The Holy Spirit will always point you to Jesus, make you more like Jesus, and help you in every way. It is time to forsake the misrepresentations of well-intentioned people who perhaps were ignorant of Him or were put off from receiving and walking in this gift because some have misused it or wrapped it in trappings that do not faithfully express God's character or nature.

The pattern in scripture reveals that after the Gentiles received salvation, they received the Holy Spirit baptism, "for they heard them speak with tongues and magnify God" (Acts 10:46, NKJV).

Rather than being ashamed of tongues, let the Holy Ghost pray through you, out loud and on purpose. The Bible states, "they heard," so don't be afraid to let them hear you pray. Make it normal because **it is normal to pray in tongues**. It has been high-jacked. If I were the devil, I would do my utmost to convince you not to pray in the Spirit. I would appeal to your intellect and pride so you wouldn't pray with stammering lips. I would not want you to discover this tool of heaven to defeat me if I were the enemy. I would work overtime making sure I hid this secret from you. It is time to bring the power back!

God sent a laborer named Ananias to Saul to pray for him *"so that you might see again and be filled to overflowing with the Holy Spirit"* (Acts 9:17, TPT). It worked. Later, we see Paul thanking God that He prays in tongues more than all the people he's around (I Corinthians 14:18). I personally believe the reason Paul wrote two-thirds of the New Testament was due to the countless hours He spent praying in tongues. Paul received revelation from the Holy Spirit.

Although the emphasis in this book is highlighting what praying in tongues—your heavenly prayer language—does for you, unless you know the person of the Holy Spirit, you will never give yourself to this amazing experience. You must get to know Him. It is like having a best friend.

MY BEST FRIEND

We all have that person we can be our real selves with. Through time spent, we come to know one another. I have known my husband for 36 years; I know him intimately. I know what he likes, dislikes, what he loves, what he is passionate about. I know his dreams, his hopes, and even his fear. He is my best friend. I know him so well that I can interpret him and know what he will do before he does it. I know his looks, mannerisms, and quirks. But even after all these years, he will still do something that intrigues me. All of a sudden, there is a new mystery, a new depth to explore, and I'm on the pursuit again. It is the same way with the Holy Spirit. He wants us to get to know Him. He is not hiding. He desires to reveal Himself to you. He wants you to know what He likes, dislikes, what He loves and is passionate about … and just when you think you can anticipate Him, a new mystery is thrown into it, beckoning further pursuit.

Holy Spirit has become to me my dearest and closest friend. He is God, and we all know about and are comfortable with the role of God as Father and God as Jesus the Son. But what about the Holy Spirit?

I grew up in the Pentecostal/charismatic movement, so I knew when one was baptized in the Holy Ghost, they spoke with other tongues as the Spirit gave them utterance. I knew the Holy Spirit gave boldness to be a witness. I received my prayer language as a young child and spoke in tongues. However, the Holy Spirit always seemed to be somewhat of a mystery. I knew He was there, but He wasn't often spoken of. He was acknowledged but not recognized.

Jesus took time to introduce the Holy Spirit to His disciples as He provided insight into His person. In fact, Jesus almost seemed excited to go away so the Holy Spirit could make His entrance in the earth. He said it was to their advantage that He go away so the Father could send the Comforter—the Helper, the Counselor—to them (John 16:7).

Have you ever had a group of friends you wanted to meet? You loved all of them and just knew they would click if they just had the opportunity to meet? I was recently blessed by an opportunity just like that. A beloved friend of mine wanted to gather several of her friends together to just hang out at a cabin for a few days and to have a meaningful connection. I thought it a rather brave idea, but she's cutting edge and bold enough to embark on a holy experiment. Several women flew in from all across the country, intrigued by the invite. She introduced us to one another, and instant connections happened. I have been blessed with new friends by my friend introducing me to hers.

I think that's how it was for Jesus. He wanted His friends that had left all to follow Him to meet Holy Spirit. Jesus knew His assignment. He had to go to the Cross and pay the ultimate price for our redemption. He had to die for our sins. He did so willingly. After three days, He was gloriously resurrected, and as a result, we are offered salvation. Jesus bought our redemption. He was then seated at the right hand of the Father in heaven (Hebrew 12:2).

God the Father and God the Son never planned to leave us alone. Not for one moment. They had planned from the foundation of the world to have God the Holy Spirit come and live inside of our born-again spirit once we received salvation. They were not going to leave us to ourselves. The Holy Spirit would live in us.

> "Now it is God who makes both us and you stand firm in Christ. He anointed us, set His seal of ownership on us, and <u>put His Spirit in our hearts</u> as a deposit, guaranteeing what is to come."
>
> 2 CORINTHIANS 1:22, NIV (EMPHASIS ADDED)

Jesus said:

> "And I will pray the Father, and He shall give you another Comforter, that He may abide with you forever—"
>
> JOHN 14:16, KJV

We need the Comforter now, just as the early apostles did then. We are not left as orphans but were entrusted to part of the Godhead to help us in the journey from here to eternity. God did not leave us on our own. He gave to us the Spirit of Truth, who would lead and guide us through perilous times (John 16:13). We have God Himself in us, praying with us and for us to ensure we fulfill our God-given purpose as well as make it safely home.

HOW JESUS DESCRIBES HOLY SPIRIT

> "And I will ask the Father, and He will give you another Helper, (Comforter, Advocate, Intercessor—Counselor, Strengthener, Standby), to be with you forever—The Spirit of Truth, whom the world cannot receive [and take to its heart] because it does not see Him or know Him, but you know Him because He (the Holy Spirit) remains with you continually and will be in you.
>
> I will not leave you as orphans [comfortless, bereaved, and helpless]; I will come [back] to you."
>
> JOHN 14:16-18, AMP

My spirit jumped in me when I read this. Throughout the process of praying in tongues, I had come to learn (and am still learning) these many facets of the Holy Spirit in varying degrees. It became more and more about the relationship as Holy Spirit pushed continually against my religious ideas.

I began to understand that I was not just some project the Holy Spirit was commissioned by the Godhead to fix; I was not a wounded waif that He was obligated to help. It was more like Jesus saying:

> "Okay, Holy Spirit, I did My part in dying to redeem her; now I entrust her to You. Show her who she really is—a child of God, not an orphan. Strip that spirit off of her and teach her to wear the robe of righteousness My blood provided.

Rid her of thoughts of independence to self-protect and self-direct and teach her to trust Us.

"Since You are the **Spirit of Truth**, *show her she is a daughter of Heaven's realm, disclose to her the beautiful relationship with Us—the Trinity—and teach her about her identity, her inheritance, and infinite worth.*

"*Be her* **Counselor** *as she struggles to trade the lie for truth at times, help her in the process and strengthen her when she wants to fall back to mediocrity rather than move the mountains that intimidate her.*

"*Be her* **Comforter**. *Comfort her when this cruel world hurts her heart with crushing pain. Wrap her in Your arms as You hold and comfort her as a mother would. Intercede for her when she cannot utter another prayer as the tears she's sobbed surrendered her soul to sleep.*

"*Be her* **Advocate** *from the evil one who has studied her, knows her weakness and propensity to the pitfalls. She will need a* **Deliverer** *from the dungeon. Defend her.*

"*Be her* **Standby**. *She will expect you to abandon her, but as she journeys with Us and just keeps letting You pray through her, this process will purge her from all that pollutes and bring forth the glorious image-bearer of the kingdom that she truly is.*

"*Holy Spirit, Father and I have entrusted You as her* **Guide**. *Show this dear one the way home in spite of the peril, temptation, and victories. She thinks You are just going to help her with a few problems; she has no idea you will transform her as you unravel her from everything she is not,* *and introduce her to Father as He really is, not what her filter has taught her.*

"You will show her the beauty and brilliance of the Sovereign King of Heaven, who she will surrender to and serve with delight as she discovers days of destiny, her eternal purpose and passion for this life and the one to come. She will have unbroken fellowship with You, and We will make her heart Our home and enjoy a delightful closeness."

You may be thinking, "If only!" I testify and do tell you the truth that this God we serve—this Holy Trinity—are all involved in the process of our redemption. God the Father, God the Son, and God the Holy Spirit long to know us and be known by us. Imagine, when we spend any time praying in the Holy Spirit, the Holy Spirit is praying God's perfect will for our lives and is committed to protecting our person in perilous times. He **will** complete the good work He has begun in us (Philippians 1:6). I have come to know the Holy Spirit in this way through the process of praying in tongues. It became about relationship, not distant religious rules. As we often say in our church, "Religion go! Holy Spirit, come!" I declare it daily. The Holy Spirit wants to come.

The next chapter will look briefly at the seven attributes Jesus revealed about the Holy Spirit.

WHEN WE SPEND ANY TIME PRAYING IN THE HOLY SPIRIT, THE HOLY SPIRIT IS PRAYING GOD'S PERFECT WILL FOR OUR LIVES.

HE **WILL** COMPLETE THE GOOD WORK HE HAS BEGUN IN US.

CHAPTER FIVE

SEVEN ATTRIBUTES OF THE HOLY SPIRIT

"And I will ask the Father, and He will give you another Helper, (Comforter, Advocate, Intercessor—Counselor, Strengthener, Standby), to be with you forever—the Spirit of Truth, whom the world cannot receive [and take to its heart] because it does not see Him or know Him, but you know Him because He (the Holy Spirit) remains with you continually and will be in you.

I will not leave you as orphans [comfortless, bereaved, and helpless]; I will come [back] to you."

JOHN 14:16-18, AMP

Jesus describes the Holy Spirit as our:

- Comforter
- Counselor
- Helper
- Intercessor
- Advocate
- Strengthener
- Standby

COMFORTER

Webster's 1828 Dictionary defines comforter as:

1. *One who administers comfort or consolation; one who strengthens and supports the mind in distress or danger. 2. The title of the Holy Spirit, whose office is to comfort and support the Christian.*

I have experienced times when the Holy Spirit has comforted me. We all remember 2020. If it wasn't bad enough to deal with a global pandemic, it was also the year my dad died, followed by a dear friend of 32 years who also died unexpectedly. Wave after wave of disappointment and grief washed over me, but it was also the year I came to know Holy Spirit as Comforter in a new way. It changed my whole periphery. I contended with such a feeling of loss—loss of my dad, loss of my friend, loss of control, loss of identity, loss of routine, loss of rhythm. I was having a hard time sleeping which compounded everything. I just hurt on the inside. That is the only way I could describe it.

Until I went through this season, I did not realize to the degree I did not know Holy Spirit as Comforter. Through the process of grieving, I experienced Him in a new way. He showed up through people. I discovered the kindness of God through Holy Spirit. His ministry always points us to Jesus, who takes us to our Real Dad, Father God. During this time, my daughter had a puppy who would not leave my side. I would sit in my backyard with my journal and Bible. Mostly I would cry. The puppy would just look at me. I felt the Holy Spirit gently whisper, "I am like that; I am not going to leave you. I am with you in this. I will carry you through. I am here. This grief is necessary to heal. I can handle you hurting, and it won't always be this way." I know it sounds strange, but I experienced His comfort as I never had before. It was a soothing balm to my soul. Each day got better. Little did I know, seven people would leave my life in that season, but the Holy Spirit was there tenderly carrying me.

COUNSELOR

> 1. *Any person who gives advice; but properly one who is authorized by natural relationship, or by birth, office or profession, to advise another in regard to his future conduct and measures. 2. The members of a counsel; one appointed to counsel a king or chief magistrate in regard to the administration of the government (1828 Dictionary).*

Holy Spirit has been my Counselor in all areas of my life: finances, relationships, and business. His counseling is free of charge. He is wisdom and will provide the understanding necessary to implement knowledge. When I do not know what to do, I sit down and say, "Holy Ghost, I need some wisdom on this situation. Would

You counsel me and give me understanding?" Then I will spend time praying in the Spirit until I get an answer.

I have learned not to move forward until I have His peace and direction. He has counseled me around some pitfalls. He sees perfectly. I see dimly. He makes me look smarter than I really am as He accesses the mind of Christ for me. He has counseled me where and when to buy property and to whom to sell it. I am not a realtor, but I have sold several properties "by owner." He has placed me in situations I didn't belong in, only to give me a download of understanding that created room for me. I have experienced crazy favor by listening to His counsel. It has been amazing.

HELPER

1. One that helps, aids or assists; an assistant; an auxiliary. 2. One that furnishes or administers remedy (1828 Dictionary).

The Holy Spirit is my Helper. I liken Him to my Guide and Outfitter in life. He knows what I need and prepares me for the journey, assisting me to reach my destination. He accompanies me as well as provides direction. The Holy Spirit helps me in relationships. Being a people person, He has had to teach me about this. The Holy Ghost brings the right people into my life and keeps the wrong people from me even if He must remove them. He is all about relationship and wants to help me choose godly traveling companions. The Holy Spirit knows who I need to be connected to and who will be good for me. He can be trusted to knit my heart to the right people. I had to learn to pay attention to the times He nudged me on the inside.

The Holy Spirit knows if someone is not right for us or not healthy. It does not necessarily mean they are bad people; it may just be the two of you together would not call one another higher. I highly recommend putting the Holy Ghost in charge of your friend list. He will help you become a better friend and bring high-caliber people to you.

INTERCESSOR

An intercessor is a mediator; one who interposes between parties at variance, with a view to reconcile them; one who pleads on behalf of another (1828 Dictionary).

God prays for me. It is astounding to think when I couldn't even pray that the Holy Spirit prayed for me. Who is this God that He would give Himself to intercede on our behalf? Such a truth is humbling. As C.H. Spurgeon said, "Child of God, you cost Christ too much for Him to forget you."

As I was writing this book, I went through a fierce battle, the kind of battle that makes you want to hide because of hurts and hang-ups. You know the place. It is a place of retreat, the place you consider quitting, the place where you want to give up as the lies continue to grow louder than the longing. It is the place where you are living by faith in the dark, and a slip or two silences your confidence. It is a lonely place where everything you know and believe feels the opposite of the seat you now occupy. In times like that, I need a touch.

Though I am thankful for the safe people in my life, they cannot touch that place deep within for which I cannot find language. It feels desperately lonely. Regardless, I continued writing. An old wound surfaced, and God felt a million miles away. I had a choice to make. Would I say yes to another level of surrender, or would I yield to the desires that were attempting to draw me away?

My heart has always wanted God. I have longed for Him from my earliest days, but something was happening to my heart. It didn't feel as connected for whatever reason. I was still showing up, but it sure seemed shallow. There are so many distractions to assist our pulling away from God in this kind of season. My soul needed something, but I didn't know what. I opened my laptop to pen words to help others in the battle, to corral courage to continue on in the journey ... that is when it happened. As I started typing, the Holy Spirit began to hover. I felt His tangible presence. I began to weep. He had come. I couldn't contain it any longer. I left the keyboard and found myself on my face in my prayer room sobbing as the Spirit began to pray through me, for me. He hovered. I broke. A dam of pent-up pain erupted from within. The torrent of emotions flooded through; grief over so many who were dear to me that died, pain from betrayal, from people leaving the faith, the pressure of ministry, the fear, the uncertainty, my weakness, my sin ...

His presence came and with a force that cleansed, healed, and delivered. I laid before Him, humbled that He came. He had missed me as much as I missed Him. I was desperate for Him. I told Him that I chose Him all over again. I want to walk how He wants me to walk. I want to walk worthy of my calling. I'm thankful He lives in me, but oh how I want Him to come upon me. He wanted my companionship as much as I wanted His. When I did not have the words to pray, He came alongside me and interceded for me. It was a breath of fresh air.

ADVOCATE

To advocate means to plead in favor of; to defend by argument, before a tribunal; to support or vindicate (1828 Dictionary).

The Holy Spirit advocates on our behalf. When we utter those syllables before God, it is causing great favor to come upon our lives as we pray for the mysteries. I recall a season in my life where I was learning not to defend myself. I think this is extremely difficult for all of us. I have a background of abuse, and these kinds of experiences lead you to believe no one will stand up for you, and, as a result, you become your own defender. I was very defensive. I felt I had to justify everything if I was accused of anything. I had to prove my innocence. I needed someone who would advocate for me and defend me.

A time comes to mind when the Holy Spirit whispered to my heart, "You know what your life looks like with you defending it. How about turning that over to Me? Allow Me to advocate for you. I will vindicate. When you defend yourself, you limit Me and make yourself look guilty. Let Me be your defender." I cannot tell you the burden that lifted when I surrendered my rights to the Advocate. I started walking in a different place.

STRENGTHENER

Strengthener is that which increases strength, physical or moral (1828 Dictionary).

I recall times when I just felt I was done and could not go on. Then suddenly, I got a second wind. The Strengthener showed up on the scene. His strength is made perfect in our weakness (2 Corinthians

12:8-10). He knows we cannot do it on our own, and the good news is, we are not expected to. He wraps our weakness in His strength and ability, swallowing it up in might. He gives us the grace to do what we cannot do in our own ability. The Holy Spirit—the Strengthener—is God's ability moving through us, doing for us what we cannot do in our own strength.

STANDBY

> 1. A staunch supporter or adherent; one who can be relied upon. 2. Something upon which one can rely and therefore choose or use regularly (Dictionary.com).

Holy Ghost is the Standby. He stands by me when the world walks away, or a friend betrays. He stands by me regardless of the kind of day, week, or month I am having. He doesn't leave my side regardless of my mood or attitude. He is faithful even when I am not. He does not break the covenant, but He contends for me to stand. I think sometimes He is just hoping I will employ Him—choose to access and use regularly—and begin to pray so He can speak order to chaos. Whether or not I turn Him loose, He is standing by.

THE HOLY SPIRIT IS TOO SECURE TO FEEL REJECTED, AND HE PATIENTLY WATCHES AS WE TRY TO FILL THE VOID OUTSIDE OF HIM WITH SILLY SUBSTITUTES

He is too secure to feel rejected, so He patiently watches as I sometimes try to fill the void outside of Him with silly substitutes. He is in a state of readiness to act and can be relied upon as He is ever faithful. An example I will share about Holy Spirit as Standby was when we had an entire community come against us as people and a ministry when our church attempted to buy a building to house our growing church. We had the money, the building was for sale, and we made an offer. All hell broke loose. The community was in an uproar. We were the unfortunate recipients of social media slander and harassment, our church van had the tires slashed, and they even posted our house address and pictures of our daughter. Even the local politicians told us our church would never be in that prime piece of real estate. Attorneys were involved. We were the talk of the town. We would enter a store, and everyone stopped and stared. The good works we were known for were erased from the collective mind of the community. It felt awful to be misunderstood, misrepresented, and have people forsake us. It was a lonely time.

Our church continued steadfast in prayer—we prayed in tongues individually and corporately. The members honored our request not to enter the fight but to pray and fast with us. There was no let-up. We made the paper. The persecution was so bad that eventually, the *Philadelphia News* came to the suburbs to do a story on this church that would need a miracle from God. Yes, we made the paper and the news! I cannot describe how awful that felt, but I can tell you the Holy Spirit stayed right next to us. He was our Standby. He was proud to stand by us. He wasn't slinking in the shadows, ashamed. He stands when the crowd leaves. Let me tell you what our Standby did for us. As a result of being on the news, the very next day, a woman called our office and said she saw on the local news that we needed a church building. They were closing theirs and wanted to know if we wanted to buy it! We went to look at the property that morning, and by that afternoon, we had an offer down on the beautiful five-acre campus. It was a better property in a nicer part of town. When a whole community stepped away, the Standby stepped up and showed off!

A FRIEND WITH BENEFITS

When we enter into a relationship with the Person of the Holy Spirit, we get to experience all His attributes. He is a friend that comes with many benefits! I absolutely believe God says good things about us. I think it would astound us if we knew His thoughts and the conversations Heaven has concerning His people. I also believe we can be a part of those conversations.

> "I still have many things to say to you, but you are not able to bear them or to take them upon you or to grasp them now. But when He, the Spirit of Truth (the Truth-giving Spirit) comes, He will guide you into all the Truth (the whole, full Truth). For He will not speak His own message [on His own authority]; but He will tell whatever He hears [from the Father, He will give the message that has been given to Him], and He will announce and declare to you the things that are to come [that will happen in the future]. He will honor and glorify Me, because He will take of (receive, draw upon) what is Mine and will reveal (declare, disclose, transmit) it to you."
>
> JOHN 16:12-14, AMPC

I find it mind-blowing that I can have access to the mind of Christ and that the Holy Spirit would transmit to me what I need to know, revealing the plans of heaven for my life is astounding. How does the Holy Spirit do this? I believe the answer is found in 1 Corinthians 14:2, which says:

> "For he who speaks in a tongue does not speak to men but to God, for no one understands him; however, in the Spirit he speaks mysteries" (NKJV).

> "For one who speaks in an [unknown] tongue speaks not to men but to God, for no one understands or catches his meaning, because in the [Holy] Spirit he utters secret truths and hidden things [not obvious to the understanding]" (AMPC).

When we pray in tongues—in our personal prayer language—we speak mysteries to God. Mind you, it is a mystery to us, but not to God, and at the proper time, He will unveil to us what we have been praying. Before the foundation of the earth, God had planned for us. We are not a surprise to Him. In fact, He even knows the number of hairs on our head. A God this detailed clearly created us with purpose. The psalmist speaks about a book written with all of our days in it:

> "Your eyes have seen my unformed substance; and in Your book were all written the days that were appointed for me, when as yet there was not one of them [even taking shape]."
>
> PSALM 139:16, AMP

Wait! There is a book written about my life? I certainly want to access it and discover why God sent me from eternity to time. When we spend time edifying ourselves by praying in tongues, we speak those mysteries, and when we have prayed out the mystery, the revealing takes place.

I have stumbled onto what were amazing business deals. It was almost accidental and effortless, but I knew all that was happening was that I caught up to the prayers I had been praying in the Spirit. This is a grace we enter into. We are joint-heirs with Christ but also co-laborers together in the Gospel. We absolutely cannot do what only God can do; however, He will not do for us what we are supposed to do. Holy Spirit is not going to force us to pray, although He is the Spirit of prayer. We always have a choice. We get to choose. That is freedom. But when we do spend the time doing our part, joy emerges as we begin to see prayer answered. We simply get a peek into the book of our life. It unfolds before us as we pray.

Ephesians 2:10 speaks to this:

> "For we are God's [own] handiwork (His workmanship), recreated in Christ Jesus, [born anew] that we may do those good works which God predestined (planned beforehand) for us [taking paths which He prepared ahead of time], that we should walk in them [living the good life which He prearranged and made ready for us to live]" (AMPC).

In the council room of Heaven, a plan for our life was devised. In the council room of hell, I believe there is a counter-plan for our life. Only the Holy Spirit can get us past all the enemy had planned for us. Nothing is a secret or a mystery for our God. The devil cannot hide in the shadows because the Holy Spirit knows everything, for He is God. The devil cannot get one over on us if we are consistently praying because Holy Spirit is outmaneuvering the enemy and working our victory out.

Romans 8:28 declares this:

> "And we know that all things work together for good to them that love God, to those who are called according to His purpose" (NKJV).

But reading it in context, it works out for good because, again, the Holy Ghost, who is the Spirit of prayer, prays and intercedes with groaning that cannot be uttered and prays according to the will of God (Romans 8:26-27). He knows what the mind of the Spirit is because He makes intercession for the saints according to the will of God. That is why it can all work together for good. When God and man are partnering together in prayer, great things happen!

I said before that the Holy Spirit is my closest and dearest friend. I long to be in a continual, abiding relationship with Him that remains unbroken. Not fits and starts. While reading the Word one day, John 16:7 exploded in my spirit off the page. It was the perfect description of the Holy Spirit:

> "However, I am telling you nothing but the truth when I say it is profitable (good, expedient, advantageous) for you that I go away. Because if I do not go away, the Comforter (Counselor, Helper, Advocate, Intercessor, Strengthener, Standby) will not come to you, [into close fellowship with you] but if I go away, I will send Him to you [to be in close fellowship with you]" (AMPC).

The Holy Spirit is the great eavesdropper of heaven. He hears what Jesus and the Father are discussing and shares it with me.

THE SPIRIT OF TRUTH

John 16:13-15 AMPC reads,

> "But when He, the Spirit of Truth (the Truth-giving Spirit) comes, He will guide you into all the Truth (the whole, full Truth). For He will not speak His own message [on His own authority]; but He will tell whatever He hears [from the Father; He will give the message that has been given to Him], and He will announce and declare to you the things that are to come

> [that will happen in the future]. He will honor and glorify Me, because He will take of (receive and draw upon) what is Mine and will reveal (declare, disclose, transmit) it to you. Everything that the Father has is Mine. That is what I meant when I said that He [the Spirit] will take the things that are Mine and will reveal (declare, disclose, transmit) it to you."

Jesus tells us that the Holy Spirit has been sent to guide us into all truth. He is the revealer of secrets. The Holy Spirit tells us what He hears Father and Jesus saying. This is incredible. He is trying to get the answer to us. Not hiding it from us so we can struggle just a little longer. He is here to help. Nothing is off-limits. He is wisdom personified.

We see in this verse that He, being the Spirit of Truth, is qualified to inoculate us against deception. And if we ever needed to be protected from deception, it is in this current day and hour in which good is being called evil and evil is being called good. The days are marked with deception, yet we have the assurance that the Holy Spirit serves as the vanguard of our lives, leading us out of every lie and into truth. Oftentimes truth hurts us before it heals us, but the Holy Spirit is Truth and will not add Himself to a lie.

The Holy Ghost is committed to truth. He will give you a witness if someone is telling the truth. I have even had Him nudge me when someone was telling a lie. But I will also add, He will not allow us to lie to ourselves or to Him either. It's important to understand that we assassinate our own character anytime we lie. God cannot bless a lie, nor will He add Himself to one. He only traffics in light and truth. The Holy Spirit is committed to helping us live boldly in the light. He is the great Sanctifier. He brings conviction of sin so that we can repent. He works a work so deep that it changes our desires. He will continually deal with us because He loves us. He is using everything in our lives to bring glory to Jesus. The issues we shun due to being uncomfortable are the very areas He will shine a light on. He ministers to our soul and calls us out of the lowlands of passivity and into a walk of power.

GRIEVE NOT THE FRIEND

The dealings of the Holy Spirit are not an indictment, but an invitation, on which to be more Christ-like as He is committed to keeping us against that day, producing a well-built life that will handle the pitfalls of failure and the traps of success. I do not want to bring sorrow to the Holy Spirit by how I live, and according to scripture, we can. He is a person. He has a personality. He has a mind, will, and emotions. He is sensitive and can be grieved (Ephesians 4:30).

Throughout the years, He has become my nearest and dearest. I need Him. I have come to know Him as my **Helper, Healer, Counselor, Wisdom, Friend, Confidant, Intercessor,** and **Standby**. He has never left my side. I discovered Him as One so tender. He didn't drive me but patiently led me out of some dark prisons, depositing His wisdom in me, so I do not revisit the darkness. He has helped me in the battle, sustaining me until the victory came. I don't have the ability to walk in victory, even on my best day, on my most prayed up, armored up day; it has never been my ability that brought any of the victories I have enjoyed. It has been God's victory. For the Father, Jesus, and Holy Spirit walk in victory. If I stay close, the victory is mine by proximity. Their victory is displayed in my life, bringing glory to God. I love Holy Spirit and desire to know

Him more and more as He reveals and glorifies Jesus. He always points me to Jesus, who then always points me to the Father.

> "And do not bring sorrow to God's Holy Spirit by the way you live. Remember, He has identified you as His own, guaranteeing that you will be saved on the day of redemption."
>
> EPHESIANS 4:30, NLT

I do not want to grieve Him, but it is also a sobering process to invite Him in and surrender to His work. It requires a death to self and a revelation of what it means to be a servant of the Most-High God. He becomes my Sovereign. I bow at His commands. But there is also a joy that cannot be explained by this process. There is a purifying and purging that brings a new level of consecration, not resulting in a posture of condescension, but rather of a calling to enter into the burden of Jesus. To quote my spiritual father, "We must die to what we want so others can get what they need. We cannot allow others to feed in us what needs to die." The only way I know this is even possible is with the help of the Holy Spirit.

The Holy Spirit is sensitive. As one who longs to walk with Him, I have had to work at this relationship as I do all the others I value. I have had to apologize for grieving Him. I hate how it feels when He stays His hand because I said something careless or unkind or if I have offended Him by reckless or sinful conduct. I immediately feel distance because I dishonored Him. He is a person. He has boundaries. There are certain things He will not stick around for. He has made that clear in the Bible. I have had to humble myself, confess my sin, repent and receive forgiveness.

We see this with King David.

> "Cast me not away from your presence and take not your
> Holy Spirit from me. Restore to me the joy of thy salvation."
>
> PSALM 51:11-12, NKJV

David had the revelation that the Holy Spirit is key to our joy. Psalm 16:11 says,

> "You will show me the path of life, in Your Presence is fullness of joy; at Your right hand are pleasures forevermore" (NKJV).

Is it any wonder joy is also a fruit of the born-again nature? It is a manifestation of the fruit of the Spirit.

AN INVITATION TO GO DEEPER

How is your relationship with the Holy Spirit? How do you view Him? Has He been some kind of mystery? Something you don't really understand? Perhaps you know about Father and definitely know about Jesus, but you have not thought much about the Holy Spirit? I pray you are encouraged to go deeper in your understanding as Holy Spirit begins to lead and guide you into all truth and that you begin to build a relationship with Him as Counselor, Friend, and Advocate as you pray out the plan God has for you by praying in tongues. He will begin to change you into a new creation. You will like the life you get to live when you start living the life you were created to live.

YOU CAN KNOW THE HOLY SPIRIT AS YOUR HELPER, HEALER, COUNSELOR, WISDOM FRIEND, CONFIDANT, INTERCESSOR, AND STANDBY.

CHAPTER SIX

BREAKING POINT

"When we pray for the Spirit's help ... we will simply fall down at the Lord's feet in our weakness. There we will find the victory and power that comes from His love."

—ANDREW MURRAY

Desperate for freedom, sleep-deprived, and anorexic, I forged ahead with my deep dive of praying in tongues daily. I worked, coached high school basketball, raised children, and tried my best to be a good wife, but things between Dave and I were stressed. We were on the verge of a couple of decisions, one of which was whether or not we would stay together. It was at that point I understood why God sent several prophetic servants to speak the

Word of the Lord to me. I was at a crossroads. To this day, I am *so* thankful I chose the Holy Spirit's path.

I had two radical encounters. Each time God intercepted me and told me to pray in the Spirit. I was desperate enough just to do it regardless of understanding it or not. Wonder filled my soul as thoughts of hope emerged.

I became curious about what would happen if I just had the courage to stay in there and pray. *What if I just turned God loose and let Him pray through me? What would happen? What if I did indeed have a destiny in Christ Jesus? What did I have to lose?* I was on the verge of losing everything anyway, so I gave myself no choice. I would just sit and pray in tongues, and it didn't make sense to me. I would set my alarm as a reminder, and most days, I could not wait to hear it. After praying for only a few minutes, my head started to scream. *I thought, My God, when is it going to stop?! I feel like my head is going to explode!* I would look at the clock and realize that only 10 minutes had gone by!

Determined, especially with this little bit of hope I was clinging to, I prayed on. I endured despite the opposition in my thoughts and emotions. My mind was chaotic. It was running wild.

As I kept showing up to prayer, I did start to notice changes. Though subtle at first, it became so noticeable that I could not ignore or dismiss it. Others were also noticing I was changing.

One day after a season of months praying in the Spirit and learning to meditate on the Word while doing some housework, I abruptly stopped. I noticed it was quiet—super quiet on the inside. My mind was calm, not racing with thoughts. I could not believe how quiet it was! The quiet was loud. There were no racing, antagonistic, or contrary thoughts roaming through my subconscious. *What is this?* I wondered. *Peace. This must be what peace feels like.* For the first time I could ever remember, there was peace and quiet calmness in my soul. It was phenomenal. To this day, I still remember the bewildered calmness with fondness. I had prayed myself into a place of peace.

At first, I thought it was too good to be true. I held my breath waiting for the other shoe to drop. But as days piled up and turned into weeks and months, I realized the darting thoughts and discord in my mind was gone. *When did that happen?* Subtle things began to drop off. Attitudes, hurts, anger, anxiety, and fear … the power of these things were losing their hold.

Transformation is a process. We do not change overnight. In fact, when I first started praying, I had hoped God would change my circumstance. I had no idea He would start working on my character that had contributed to my circumstances.

Praying in the Spirit gives God access to order our life. He has a personal plan for each of us. We access the mind of Christ when we pray in our heavenly language. The Holy Spirit knows what is hindering our walk and keeping us from God's best for us. We enter that plan by our choosing. We have been given the gift of free will. God forces Himself on no one. He wants our YES!

Praying in tongues does nothing but benefit me (1 Corinthians 14:4). Some of those benefits were being revealed, and I was changing. The dark grey cloud of oppression wasn't hanging around as much anymore. The Son was starting to shine in my daily life. Optimism began emerging as thoughts of possibility pushed through the paralysis of a painful past. I knew I had started walking in the Spirit. I was finally moving forward.

The Holy Spirit strangled some strongholds in my life. My marriage started turning around. I did not know that my husband had also started praying consistently in the Spirit. The more I prayed in tongues, the more love showed up in my walk. My countenance and conversation began to change. I became less critical of myself and my husband. If Dave annoyed or angered me, rather than responding with control and anger as I once did, now I prayed in the Spirit. After some time, I noticed I stopped being annoyed and angered. I was the one that had changed.

There is real freedom when someone else's behavior does not affect ours. The more I prayed in tongues, the more I was being transformed. It was like I was canceling out the enemy's access to the control center of my life. He couldn't just come on by and push my buttons any longer. A new woman was emerging. In my spirit-to-Spirit connection, as I prayed in tongues, the Holy Spirit eradicated sinister strongholds.

With my marriage improving, honor became easier. I believe praying in tongues is like a dimmer switch. The Holy Spirit begins to turn the lights on and will continue to do so until a point is reached where we can't handle the brightness any longer. It is a memorable moment when God shows you who you are in the full light of His truth. Thankfully, mercy is present for this meeting. It was in this season I recognized what a good man God had given me. One who was willing to walk with me through the pain and hurt of my past. Though he had not caused it, too often, he got the brunt end of my anger. I started to fall in love with my husband all over again. I realized He was God's son. I wanted to please my heavenly Father in how I treated my husband—His gift to me. That was a massive change that suddenly materialized.

You won't pray in tongues for very long before Holy Spirit, our Helper, will begin to do just that—turn the lights on. He dwells fully in our born-again spirit from the moment we receive salvation, but as we invite Him and make room for Him through praying in tongues, He will dive deep into our soul to go to work, bringing lasting change. He knows why we think as we do, the reasons for our insecurity, mistrust, hurt, independence, and rebellion. Nothing takes Him by surprise. He was there. He is the historian of our life, and He desires that we turn Him loose to pray and rewrite our story. His story. He is the pen of mercy.

As the Holy Spirit goes to work, He begins to deal with the things that hinder us. He is committed to the journey and will absolutely pray us to a place of victory.

A MIRACULOUS TRANSFORMATION

An area of marvelous transformation for me was when the Holy Spirit prayed me out of poverty. You read that right. **The Holy Ghost began to deal with my mindset about money.** No matter what we tried, we did not prosper. There was a cap over our cash. We were faithful with the little, and I do mean we had very little. The promises of God seemed to elude us.

At this point, my husband began to pray in the Spirit. In fact, Dave had the unfortunate experience of losing his job. After sending out his resumes, he decided that he would begin to pray in the Spirit as if he was at work. He set out on his eight-hour days, complete with two fifteen-minute breaks and a thirty-minute lunch, and he would pray in tongues. He did this for six weeks. I was also praying in the Spirit for several hours a day.

I would love to tell you there is a Jesus lottery in the sky. There isn't. God presents you with the opportunity to prosper. In other words, He gives you work. During this time of extensively praying in tongues, my mom stopped by with her friend. She was an older, southern woman filled with faith. We loved listening to her stories about God and all He did throughout her life. During our visit, she looked at us and said, "You have money in your backyard."

Perplexed, we asked her what she was referring to. She said, "You have that little garage in the back; you could throw a floor up top and have two studio apartments."

It was indeed an interesting idea; however, my husband's dad had just passed away, and the garage was full of his father's tools he had inherited. He mentioned it to her, but stubborn in faith and on an assignment, she said, "Build a shed."

We said nothing. We did not have money to just build a shed. We had other more pressing needs.

Not letting up, she said, "How much would it cost to build one?"

Being a project manager and builder, Dave told her, "I could build one for $400."

"I tell you what I am going to do for you," she nodded her head, "just because God told me to help you ... I am going to gift you the $400 to build a shed. Then I'm going to loan you some money to fix the studio apartments. You get them rented out, and you can pay me back. I trust you." She took out her wallet, gave Dave four Ben Franklins, and wrapped up her visit.

Dumbfounded, we headed to Home Depot and started on the God project. Dave made quick work of it. While praying in the

Holy Ghost, God showed me two single ladies to approach to rent the property. To my surprise, each was looking for a place and needed to be out by the end of the month. Needless to say, both apartments were rented, security deposits collected, and we paid our first payment to our investor within one month.

In less than five months, we paid off the loan. The apartments in our backyard were now paying our mortgage. We kept giving, saving, and praying that God would continue to show us how to prosper. During this time, He eradicated strongholds of lack and poverty in my mind. I come from humble beginnings, and I know well the pain of poverty. All these years later, I still remember that sting. In fact, I don't want to forget it. It keeps me compassionate.

I do not feel guilt for prospering to the degree I have. I am by no means wealthy, but I am blessed. I do feel that there is great responsibility with prosperity. We are to be radically generous. If we do not have the wisdom to earn the money, we will not have the wisdom to keep the money. As I continued to pray in tongues, the Holy Spirit purged poverty mindsets and powers, all the while depositing wisdom to steward well.

One of the ways I also fight poverty is to teach people about accessing the wisdom of the Holy Spirit. He is God and lives in us. He knows exactly why we can't prosper—the tangled thoughts that hold us captive and what character development needs to take place. He probes, revealing to us any greed and materialism. He shows us what has a hold of us, where insecurity, fear, and unbelief hook us. Without dealing with those areas,

> **THE HOLY SPIRIT SHOWS US WHAT HAS A HOLD OF US, WHERE INSECURITY, FEAR, AND UNBELIEF HOOK US**

money becomes a mask. God never wants us to trust in money or to love it. It is simply a tool. He goes to work to prepare us to handle money so we can steward it well. He does not mind us having money. He does not want money to have us (1 Timothy 6:10).

After the success of the apartments, I knew a shift had taken place. I was developing a mindset to win. It was an odd but welcomed new expectation.

A year later, while on a prayer walk, I was drawn to a certain house. I cringed, as it was the ugliest house on the whole block. Jokingly, I told God, "That house is so ugly, even if You gave it to me, I wouldn't want it!" I laughed and kept walking. But, I couldn't stop thinking about that hideous house. The exterior was blue, complete with bubblegum pink trim with a castle-like tower in the corner. Absolutely ghastly! The Holy Spirit, being a person, has a sense of humor. He began joking with me, saying, "Father is gonna get that house for you!"

One night while Dave and I were on the porch enjoying one another's company (this again was a massive change), Dave said, "You know what I have been thinking about and can't get off my mind?"

With wide eyes, I said, "Please don't tell me we are supposed to buy that ugly house?!"

He laughed and said, "Yes! We can buy it, fix it up and rent it!"

Regardless of how offensive the house was, we felt God leading us, so we went to the bank, and to our astonishment, the bank was selling it for just a little more than the taxes owed on it due to the condition. Though this was a surprise to us, our prayer partner and business advisor, the Holy Spirit, already knew that detail.

The same scenario was on repeat—Home Depot, here we come! In a short time, "ugly house" turned into something special. It was renovated, rented, and eventually sold for a handsome profit. I became fond of that house as it reminded me of the renovation of my house—my soul—where Holy Spirit now resided. He remodeled me as I just kept praying in tongues.

Soon after, the lady who started the whole real estate ordeal called Dave and arranged for a meeting at a seven-unit, scary apartment complex. Yes! You guessed it. God was at it again! This woman's niece owned them. They were run down, and she wanted to be rid of them. She brokered the deal that we would renovate them, and her niece would carry the loan. Unreal.

Once again, off to Home Depot, and in less than a year, all seven apartments were remodeled and rented. Can I tell you that collecting rent from ten units a month on top of working, our tax bracket changed?! We would go on to buy another house and fix and flip it as well as many other property pursuits, all the while knowing that we had tapped into praying in the Spirit who was revealing to us His plan in prospering us.

Why would a woman favor us out of all the people around her? Because she had heard from God, and He told her to help us. He told her to "Teach that young couple how to prosper." She obeyed, but we also obeyed. We saw the opportunity God was giving us. Money doesn't fix money problems. Praying in the Spirit fixed our problem with prospering.

I am convinced that God has a plan for each of our personal lives, and when we spend our time praying in the Holy Ghost, we are accessing the mind of Christ for our lives, situation, family, prosperity, wisdom, ministries, etc. He used our skillset to prosper us through real estate. Your road will look different than mine, but as you pray, He will be faithful to unfold it. He did all of this without either of us having a real estate license.

THE DIVINE MEDDLER

When we pray in tongues, the invisible strongholds are toppled. In this life, struggles do not dissipate, but there is a place in the walk of the Spirit where those struggles do not defeat and devastate, as wisdom takes its place to navigate through the problems. Strongholds no longer stop progress, even if you must stop and contend with one.

As Holy Spirit dealt with the fortress of anger and poverty, He also dealt with the bastion of lust. I will speak more on this later, but the hope is that if we continue to pray in tongues, nothing can stand under the power of the Holy Spirit praying in us, building us up on our most holy faith.

> "But you, my delightfully loved friends, constantly and progressively build yourselves up on the foundation of your most holy faith by praying every moment in the Spirit. Fasten your hearts to the love of God and receive the mercy of our Lord Jesus Christ, who gives us eternal life.
>
> "Keep being compassionate to those who still have doubts, and snatch others out of the fire to save them. Be merciful over and over to them, but always couple your mercy with the fear of God. Be extremely careful to keep yourselves free from the pollutions of the flesh.
>
> "Now to the One with enough power to prevent you from stumbling into sin and bring you faultless before His

> glorious presence to stand before Him with ecstatic delight, to the only God our Savior, through our Lord Jesus Christ, be endless glory and majesty, great power and authority—from before He created time, now, and throughout all the ages of eternity. Amen."
>
> JUDE 1:20-25, TPT

The Holy Spirit will deal with everything unholy in our lives so we can walk worthy of the calling (Ephesians 4:1).

Due to childhood sexual abuse, a fortress of lust had taken up residence within me. I love God as Father, God as Son, and God as Holy Spirit because the blessed, unified Trinity approaches the dirty and unclean places in me to save, cleanse, heal, and deliver. Satan wants us to hide in shame and secrecy as He accuses us. As I prayed and continued to pray in the Spirit, even when condemned by my thoughts, I knew if I would just stay in there, I would be transformed. I had to believe my desires would change. I was not a leper. I was a wounded woman that needed oil and wine poured on her wounds. I needed my soul restored. Holy Spirit was my good Samaritan who did just that. He was a kind Comforter, nurturing my needs and speaking to my true identity. Over time, healing came. Holiness held. Though the battle can still rage at times, the battle is on the outside, not the inside. That was a game-changer.

Jesus speaks of Holy Spirit as rivers of living water.

> "Then on the most important day of the feast, the last day, Jesus stood and shouted out to the crowds—'All you thirsty ones, come to Me! Come to Me and drink! Believe in Me so that rivers of living water will burst out from within you, flowing from your innermost being just like the Scripture says.'

> "Jesus was prophesying about the Holy Spirit that believers were prepared to receive. But the Holy Spirit had not yet been poured out upon them, because Jesus had not yet been unveiled in His full splendor."
>
> JOHN 7:37-39, TPT

He is a river of refreshing, a fountain that never runs dry. As a kid, on a hot summer day, we would run for the river by our house. It was refreshing, fun, and playful. It was Jesus who referenced a river when introducing Holy Spirit. How would it change us to think of Him as refreshing, fun, even playful?

> "There is a river whose streams make glad the city of God, the holy habitation of the Most High."
>
> PSALM 46:4, ESV

These streams are rivers that flow from the Holy Spirit's heart, and it makes me glad.

In my quest of praying in tongues and after years of faithfully praying in the Spirit, there was a season when I fell out of this practice. It was difficult. I resorted to leaning on my own understanding, and I soon grew frustrated. I live by fire in my belly, and I missed praying and communing with God as I was accustomed.

Holy Spirit gently reminded me that praying in the Spirit is a grace. It is not a legalistic requirement. It is not a box to be checked. It is not a discipline to be performed to be a good Christian. Praying in the Holy Ghost is a gift wrapped in grace. It is something into which I am invited.

If you have never tried praying in tongues, or if you have fallen out of this practice, I encourage you just to jump in. Start the conversation. There is no condemnation; just start praying. Holy Spirit is your Helper and will pick up right where you left off. He is the Spirit of prayer. Pray on!

PRAYING IN THE HOLY GHOST IS A GIFT WRAPPED IN GRACE.

CHAPTER SEVEN

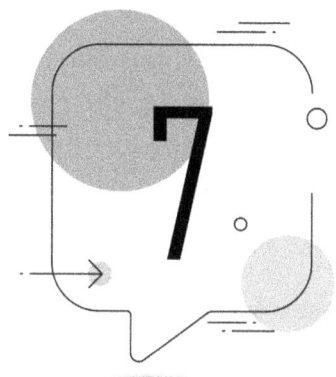

SURVIVING THE PURGE

"Revelation is the first step to holiness, and consecration is the second. A day must come in our lives, as definite as the day of our conversion, when we give up all right to ourselves and submit to the absolute Lordship of Jesus Christ."

—WATCHMAN NEE

I've often said, "If you can be stopped, you will be stopped!" There is a dogged determination required to stay in there with the Holy Ghost and continue to pray. Most of us are motivated to start out praying for our circumstances to get better while the Godhead is at work on our character.

The Holy Spirit is committed to our transformation. He desires to make us like Jesus. But any honest person will admit that there are times when we are anything but Christ-like. It could be in an attitude, thought, reaction, or deed. The truth is, we often rely on our will to behave, or we attempt to modify our actions rather than experience true transformation. I was looking for a permanent change. It is exhausting to try to "just behave."

Exhausting and not sustainable.

We are all looking for help to change. Self-help books line the bookshelves. We all have character flaws we do not like in ourselves but have no idea how to get rid of them, so we live frustrated or in a cycle of "try harder" or throw ourselves into rigorous religious activity.

God never intended us to live frustrated lives. He wants us to prosper and be in good health (3 John 2). He gave us the Holy Spirit to reveal the mysteries of Christ Jesus in us and to bring change through the edification process. But, it isn't always an easy process because there are no quick fixes or shortcuts to lasting change.

When the Holy Spirit is edifying us and helping us understand the revelation of the Word, He is also working in our born-again spirit to provide strength to put to death the deeds of the flesh, those areas that war against our soul.

When we abide in Jesus and bear fruit, He said, He would prune (or purge) the fruit so we can bear more fruit (John 15:2). When we don't bear fruit, we also get pruned. It's the "pruned if you do, pruned if you don't" scenario.

When I share about praying in tongues, I can see the excitement of hope as they know their lives will change. I can sense they think it will be a quick-fix, almost like a magical formula. The truth is, it is slower than we like, and an internal war is about to be embarked upon if you consistently pray in tongues. Consistent prayer applies pressure on every area that needs surrender. Impurities rise to the surface of the soul that we may not wish to address. Sometimes we have wrapped our identity around our issues for so long that we aren't sure who we might be without them. This can be a terrifying thought! But God persists in going after the layers life has put on us to purge them so we can fulfill our call and so the devil can't destroy us. The Holy Spirit will perfect change.

He deals with the dead things clinging to us as we abide in the vine. These things serve to cap us and prevent us from going higher or deeper. Have you ever tried to move out and do something for God, and the devil stops you through finances, wrong motives, or sinful heart attitudes? These are the types of things the Holy Spirit wants to purge from us. If we don't allow Him to cleanse us of these things, then the devil has successfully kept us contained. This is not the will of God for any of us. Just as the Holy Spirit enlightens us to the mysteries of God in Christ, He also strengthens our born-again spirit to survive the purge.

ONE THING AT A TIME

The Holy Spirit does not purge us of everything all at once. We could not handle that. He waits until we have built ourselves up on our faith by praying in the Spirit. It is then He knows we can handle the war our soul will go through (emotions and thoughts) when He starts to uproot and purge that issue from our soul. We are not left to ourselves to perform this task as we simply cannot change ourselves. We have the Holy Spirit's ministry to help us.

Romans 8:13 says,

> "For if ye live by the flesh, ye shall die:
> but if ye through the Spirit do mortify the
> deeds of the body, ye shall live" (KJV).

When you pray in the Spirit consistently, you will undergo a purging process. It is not fun; it is necessary. To be forewarned is a blessing. He simply must purge from our lives the dead things that prevent us from living the abundant life Jesus came to give. He doesn't come to point out my faults but rather what needs to be purged because it does not serve His purpose or my good.

The mysteries we pray out in tongues are for our benefit, not the Holy Spirit's. We are praying the mysteries of Christ in us, the hope of glory, and as we pray, the Holy Spirit turns on the lights. His glorious light is devoid of darkness, and in the brilliance of His illumination, our blindness lifts. We see the spiritual roadblocks, sins, shortcomings, faults, and pride that keep us from progressing in our walk with God, and we must cling to His mercy, trusting by faith that we can be this fully known and still fully loved.

When the Holy Spirit turned the lights on in my broken soul, rather than a floodlight blinding me, His brightness came more like a dimmer switch. He gave me only as much light as I could handle. It was gradual and wrapped in grace.

Admittedly, it was daunting to look at the mess with Him as I would gaze around the various rooms in my soul. I was almost relieved to see what it was I kept tripping over. I was tired of being defeated when my will would betray me, and my emotions would hijack my good efforts to be like Jesus.

The day I decided to turn the Holy Ghost loose and let Him pray through me, I made a dedicated decision not to quit regardless of the emotional strongholds I might come up against. It was a decision that would determine my destiny. I yielded to a process I did not completely understand. For six months, I prayed for two hours. I didn't miss a day. Mostly, I did not feel like doing it, but I was so rather tired of the devil jerking my chain anytime he wanted to through circumstances, people, or my emotions, that I was willing to do it.

I consciously hid in Christ and surrendered to Holy Spirit to pray through me the perfect will of God for my life, uttering the mysteries of Christ. I was communicating before God's throne every time I prayed in tongues.

I was tired of the enemy of my soul tormenting me, dragging his creepy hand through my life, discovering what he could hook me with just because he wanted to. That was infuriating. The enemy is cunning, and he'll keep at it until he finds out what works. He was and is the author of every violation, abuse, and injustice. He has studied us and knows our weaknesses and propensities. I **know** Jesus stopped him at Calvary, but I needed the experiential knowledge of the positional truth applied to my life. I needed to possess in my person what Jesus purchased for me. It is one thing to read about victory; it is another to live it. I wanted to live it out loud—bold and on purpose.

I desired the work in me to be so complete that when the devil came knocking on my door, a different woman answered. I wanted to destroy the enemy's access to the control center of my life. The Holy Ghost did too.

As I prayed in tongues, it was as if the Holy Ghost began to deal with the dam in my soul, log by log. In His wisdom, He started to remove the logs at the top, whereas I, in my impatience, would have gone for the lynchpin. He knows how to handle us! He has perfect knowledge of us. He has all the classified information on us, and He uses it to heal and help us, not to find fault. He is aware of what broke us, why we react to things the way we do, our struggles, weaknesses, and battles. He also knows our strengths, gifts, talents, and fortitude. He understands and is a merciful and kind God. He does not break the broken; He does not wound the wounded. He restores, but it is a process.

> "For we do not have a High Priest who is unable to sympathize and understand our weaknesses and temptations, but One who has been tempted [knowing exactly how it feels to be human] in every respect as we are, yet without [committing any] sin. Therefore let us [with privilege] approach the throne of grace [that is, the throne of God's gracious favor] with confidence and without fear, so that we may receive mercy [for our failures] and find [His amazing] grace to help in time of need [an appropriate blessing, coming just at the right moment]."
>
> HEBREWS 4:15-16 AMP

To see God in this light is most helpful as the Holy Spirit will come to sift us because He loves us. He prunes us, so we bear more fruit (John 15:2). We need to survive the purge as He purifies our heart.

DON'T GIVE UP

When we pray in tongues, it is only a matter of time until we will run into a position or situation from which there is no escape—an impasse—a place we have never gotten past. A perusal of your family tree may reveal that this has stopped everyone in your bloodline. This is the place where your thoughts and emotions gang up on you, and it seems progress is no longer possible. You just want to quit. You feel like you cannot continue praying any longer, and to top it off, you just don't care anymore! There is tension and conflict inside, and it feels like nothing alleviates the pressure. In fact, the more you pray, the worse it seems to get.

An impasse is a place where those before you more than likely settled. They also couldn't get past it. As the Spirit works in you, you may become acquainted with a bit more understanding, mercy, and grace as you no longer judge your ancestors.

Pray in the Spirit long enough, and you will eventually find yourself here. Those in your bloodline may not have known what you are discovering. You have a way to pray yourself out of this mess, and the Holy Ghost wants to help you. Lay judgment down and step into the freedom God desires for you.

Show up and speak the mysteries of the prayer Holy Spirit supplies. He will continue shining the light. Jesus said:

> "For there is nothing hid, which shall not be manifested;
> neither was anything kept secret, but
> that it should come abroad."
>
> MARK 4:22, KJV

Jesus is the light of the world. The Holy Spirit continues the ministry of Jesus in our lives, and when we pray in the Spirit, the light grows brighter and brighter. Father, Son, and Spirit all walk through the rooms of our soul and turn the lights on everything hidden. Our flesh does not like its deeds exposed, preferring to stay back and slink in the shadows, hiding in the comfort of darkness.

Be encouraged; God is at work. Transformation within **is** taking place. Don't quit praying in tongues consistently if change does not manifest quickly. Realize that if it took decades to get into the condition we are in, it's may take some time to live out change and walk in freedom. Do not give up before God is finished.

Even though I felt what I came from was too disgraceful and would eventually cause me to implode and derail, Holy Spirit gave me His hand. It was an invitation. He showed me I could trust Him to pray me through it. I placed my hand in the hand of the One that could pray me past all the impasses and change my life. It really was possible that I could live the abundant life Jesus died to give me.

POWER TO CHANGE

I can tell you now that the grace of God has so transformed my life that when people hear my story, they think I'm lying. Truly the pen of mercy has rewritten my life. The contribution of Jude is profound as he encourages us to pray in the Holy Ghost and build ourselves up on our most holy faith. But notice what we are building ourselves up from:

> "They used to say to you, 'In the last days there will be scoffers, following after their own ungodly passions.'

> "These are the ones who are [agitators] causing divisions—worldly-minded [secular, unspiritual, carnal, merely sensual—unsaved], devoid of the Spirit.
>
> "But you, beloved, build yourselves up on [the foundation of] your most holy faith [continually progress, rise like an edifice higher and higher], pray in the Holy Spirit, and keep yourselves in the love of God, waiting anxiously and looking forward to the mercy of our Lord Jesus Christ [which will bring you] to eternal life.
>
> "And have mercy on some, who are doubting; save others, snatching them out of the fire; and on some have mercy but with fear, loathing even the clothing spotted and polluted by their shameless immoral freedom.
>
> "Now to Him who is able to keep you from stumbling or falling into sin, and to present you unblemished [blameless and faultless] in the presence of His glory with triumphant joy and unspeakable delight, to the only God our Savior, through Jesus Christ our Lord, be glory, majesty, dominion, and power, before all time and now and forever. Amen."
>
> JUDE 1:18-25, AMP

He builds us up past our sensual nature, our "flesh." Strongholds are built in our minds, constructed by our belief systems across time. These are typically empowered by a strong emotion attached to the framework of our thoughts.

In my case, one stronghold was a fear of failure. Yet, I had experienced a measure of success in most things I attempted. But when you feel like a failure, it does not matter how many times you ace a test; even with a 4.0 GPA, you can feel stupid. I lived with a constant sense of failure looming around the corner. The Holy

Spirit crucifies, mortifies, and purges us from dead things in our lives. I prayed in the Holy Spirit enough that He enlightened me to a generational curse. I appropriated the Cross and saw the reversal of this stronghold resulting in blessing.

The Holy Spirit also deals with our love walk and makes room for His gifts to begin to flow through us. His gifts are meant to flow through a vessel of love to bless the world around us. But scripture is quite clear; it does not matter how many gifts manifest through us; the greatest is love, *agape* love, the God kind of love. Without it, we are just a bunch of noise (1 Corinthians 13).

You won't pray in the Spirit very long before He starts to go after what He is really after—for us to walk in love towards one another. He will reveal and remove hindrances in our love walk. The Word admonishes us to pray in the Holy Ghost to "guard and keep ourselves in the love of God" (Jude 1:21). Praying in the Spirit is the key to walking in love and overcoming all that would hinder us from doing so. What a gift we have been given!

The book of Jude corresponds to the book of Acts. When believers received the Holy Ghost, they were empowered to be a witness. This shows us in detail how to evangelize. There is a Holy Ghost strategy available to us. When the Holy Spirit moves through us as He did in Acts, believers are added to the church daily! The Holy Spirit prepares us as God's chosen vessel, releasing His gifts through us to help us win lost souls for Jesus.

Throughout scripture, we see God always used clean vessels. Why? His power is so fierce that He does not want the vessel destroyed when His power flows through it. He desires us to live as consecrated people sanctified for His service. This process of sanctification requires us to turn into different people—new people. Praying consistently in the Holy Ghost helps us with this purifying process.

We cannot keep ourselves. We cannot discipline ourselves against our problems with a strong will. It will eventually give way. The answer is allowing the Holy Spirit to lead us out of patterns and systems of thought that enslave us.

MODIFIED OR TRANSFORMED?

As I continued to pray in tongues, the Holy Ghost shined the light brightly, and my spiritual blindness lifted as I began to see and understand things I did not see before. When I learned how to release the power of the Holy Ghost on the inside of me, I was able to put to death the deeds of the flesh—mortification. I like the word mortification. It sounds exactly like its operation—gruesome yet glorious.

The Holy Ghost rose up on the inside of me and dealt a death blow to the hold the flesh had on me. Sin no longer has dominion over me; through the Spirit, I have dominion over sin.

In *Webster's 1828 Dictionary*, one definition of the word mortification is this:

> *In scripture, (mortification is) the act of subduing the passions and appetites by penance, abstinence, or painful severities inflicted on the body. The mortification of the body by fasting has been the practice of almost all nations, and the mortification of the appetites and passions by self-denial is always a Christian duty.*

When Holy Spirit starts the mortification process, antagonistic emotions often erupt. This is normal. Stay the course.

Mortification goes beyond the type of behavior modification with which we are familiar—the direct changing of unwanted behavior by means of biofeedback or conditioning. We may better identify it as the wonderful quality we possess to know how to behave, exhibit self-control, and respect boundaries. Behavior modification is what we do in spite of what we feel like doing, minding our manners, so to speak. While this is normal and expected in polite society, behavior modification alone is insufficient when living by and in the Spirit.

> THE HEART OF CHRISTIANITY IS THE POWER OF RELATIONSHIP WITH GOD, NOT A SET OF RULES FOCUSED ON BEHAVIOR MODIFICATION

Too often, Christianity is experienced through a paradigm of rule-keeping rather than the glorious, beautiful relationship with God that it is. Due to *religion*, we could miss the power of friendship with God and reduce it to a set of rules focusing on behavior modification.

Jesus paid the horrific price at Calvary when He died on the Cross, willingly paying the penalty for our sins. He became our substitute so we could be born again, passing from spiritual death to life. When we receive Christ, we become children of God. There is a nature change.

We literally leave the kingdom of darkness and are delivered into the kingdom of Light (Colossians 1:13). Jesus' sacrifice made peace between God the Father and us. We are no longer orphans—we are sons and daughters.

Our life changes as a result of a true born-again experience; there is a cleansing in our conduct. Scripture does deal with behavior. You may be familiar with the "what to do" and "what not to do" lists in which we all fall short. However, there is more to a walk of sanctification (being set apart) than only **conduct cleansing**. There is also **character cleansing** and a deeper work of **core cleansing**.

The Holy Spirit's work in us through mortification leads us into more and more freedom.

We don't have to rely on the mere strength of our will but can lean on and trust His work to mortify the deeds of the flesh by the Spirit (Romans 8:13). The Holy Ghost is in charge of this process. When we try to discipline ourselves against a problem, it does not result in lasting change. You cannot use flesh to deal with flesh as a permanent solution. Will power is not enough. We need Holy Ghost power. Through the Spirit and God's Word, we mortify the deeds of the body—fear, hurts, hang-ups, and habits. These all keep us in a perpetual cycle of defeat, but God's Spirit is how we break through the ceiling over our life and call.

Mortification is not a word we hear much in casual conversation, but as someone who grew up in the church and read the King James Version of the Bible, it is not unfamiliar to me.

Were you to do a word study, you would learn that to mortify means "to put to death." God mortified our sins through the death of His Son, Jesus. As believers, we are to answer this benevolent act of God by mortifying (putting to death) the "deeds of the body."

Through the power of God's Spirit, we mortify the flesh—put to death our desire for sin because our love for God burns so hot and strong that we desire Him above all else. The Spirit reigns supreme in our lives. We cannot do this on our own; we need the ministry of the Holy Ghost to rise up and defeat what is defeating us.

- Will you partner with the Holy Ghost?
- How deep will you go?
- Where will you stop and pitch a tent?
- Will you settle for the territory you now occupy, or will you continue to ascend the Mount of the Lord?

I challenge you to reach for more, even during challenging times. Ask yourself what you are after:

- Behavior modification or transformation?
- Process or performance?
- Religion or relationship?
- Audition or authenticity?

CHOOSE CONSECRATION

> "Beloved friends, what should be our proper response to God's marvelous mercies? To surrender yourselves to God to be His sacred, living sacrifice. And live in holiness, experiencing all that delights His heart. For this becomes your genuine expression of worship."
>
> ROMANS 12:1, TPT

Surrendering to the process of being sifted and purged takes intentionality. Becoming a living sacrifice and living in holiness is not a casual commitment.

God goes to the hard-to-reach places. Remain in prayer. Do not fall out of the habit of praying in tongues. You will experience lasting freedom in areas that have defeated you over and over. You will see yourself in light of His glory as you fall on His mercy.

What He shows you about yourself is truth. Receive His grace—not to excuse your condition but grace to be changed.

There is a difference between not doing something and not wanting to do it. I have often said, "Just because we don't do it; does not mean we are free." I want lasting freedom, where sin has no hold on me. I cannot endure the constant exertion of self-discipline and strength of will required to control my behavior against a problem.

Conduct, character, and core cleansing all are part of the deeper work of consecration. It takes all three. A focus on conduct alone is a religious trap. It is the path to living as a Pharisee. The Holy Spirit alone knows how to deal with our flesh, refine our character, and restore our core identity in a way that results in glorious transformation. Consecration is a painful but powerful process that is also priceless. There is glory on the other side.

During the purge, we begin to see things as God sees them. When we see His holiness, we know that we need the work of mortification. We may be saved but are we dead to sin? Is our spirit alive and free?

Praying in tongues as a daily discipline can be hard. Your mind will wander (and wonder). Some days it will pour forth like a river, and your spirit will soar in God's presence. Other days, it will feel as if an elephant is sitting on your chest. No flow. You can begin to think you're crazy for even doing it. But if you just keep uttering those syllables, faithfully praying the mysteries, transformation occurs.

Act in faith. Trust. Build yourself up past all the stuff that stopped you. Your spirit is becoming stronger as the power of the Holy Ghost purges that garbage out. Stay in there! Don't quit! Stay in the battle, take heart, and place your hand in the hand of the Holy Ghost and ask Him to get you through it. He is committed and does not back away from us in the process of our transformation, ever.

God longs to fellowship with us, and He desires us to let Him pray through us, for us, and with us regardless of our condition. He knows if we are with Him long enough, we won't stay the same. It is impossible. Jesus always changes what He touches. He couldn't leave the blind man blind, or the lame man crippled; He comes on the scene of our life through the Holy Spirit and changes us.

Turn the Holy Spirit loose to change you on the inside. Pray past it, and you will have traversed to the place where none before you were able to go. Allow God to lay His axe to the root so you can overcome. You will break through the impasse; you will overcome by the grace and glory of God. As you hold out for the victory, victory will come.

Be stubborn in prayer. Keep showing up. Do not quit. Aren't you curious to know what would happen if you turned the Holy Ghost loose to pray?

> "Direct me, Yahweh, throughout my journey
> so I can experience Your plans for my life.
> Reveal the life-paths that are pleasing to You."
>
> PSALM 25:4, TPT

CHAPTER EIGHT

THE CALL TO THE NORTHEAST

"Don't worry when you meet opposition for obeying God. Worry when you don't have opposition, because you're probably not obeying God."

—CRAIG GROESCHEL

I married an east coast boy. Dave visited the Colorado Rockies and found himself at a revival service where he gave his heart to Jesus. He decided to move to Denver and start a new life. After church one day, he asked me if I wanted to go out for "kauwfee." I liked his accent and said, "Yes!" We became fast friends. We both loved Jesus, and we would spend our time witnessing together.

I was very evangelistic, and our church did outreaches on the streets. I found out Dave had a couple of black belts, so I wanted him on my team because I was fearless. I witnessed to anything that moved, so protection was wisdom. We made a great team.

Before too long, he proposed to me, but with this full disclosure, "When I got saved," he said, "God told me one day He would send me back where I'm from to plant a church."

I answered, "Well, God spoke to me when I was a little girl that I would marry a preacher and be one myself." We got married, started a family, and pursued ministry. It was a journey of twenty years before we would be sent to the east coast to start a church, but the day arrived when a dozen people met in our living room for our first service.

I have lived in six different states, been to several continents, and I will tell you there is no place like the Northeast. I love where I live and labor. But regarding the things of the Holy Spirit, this area was desolate and barren.

When I would approach people and share the Gospel, they would just stare at me. We continued to pray in the Spirit over the region for a breakthrough. Slowly, we began to see people come to believe in Jesus as Savior. We baptized them and then approached the subject of being baptized in the Holy Ghost. I generally received the same reply as the Apostle Paul in the book of Acts:

> "... (Paul) asked them, 'Did you receive the Holy Spirit when you believed?' They answered, 'No, we have not even heard that there is a Holy Spirit.'"
>
> ACTS 19:2, NIV

I would do as Paul did: explain the gift, and just like then:

> "And when Paul (Teresa) had laid his (her) hands on them, the Holy Spirit came on them, and they began speaking in tongues and prophesying."
>
> ACTS 19:6, ESV (PERSONALIZATION ADDED)

We found that we had moved to a very "religious" region. It is a place where things have been done a certain way for hundreds of years with the understanding, "don't rock the boat." But we led a group of people called to contend for a territory to go from religion to relationship; we could not help but rock the boat. Throughout the region, the religious community talks of the Trinity—Father, Son, and Holy Ghost—yet has no understanding of the person of the Holy Spirit.

We came on the scene and started telling anyone who would listen that they could have a personal relationship directly with Father God because of Jesus dying for their sins. They only had to believe and receive. It didn't have to be a crowded relationship; it didn't have to include another person (like a priest), a bunch of rules and works, and the best part—**they could be filled with the Holy Spirit,** whose whole job was to assist and help them in their walk of faith.

We truly have had to contend for a breakthrough in the territory. Praying in the Holy Spirit dealt with the spiritual climate. Despite no response, our team continued to treat it as a mission field. We had a great group of Jesus-loving people who would contend for the faith. We continued in prayer, worship, and confessing what the Word said over the region. We added fasting. We knew we needed a breakthrough that only heaven could bring. The Holy Spirit had to begin to breathe upon the hearts of men and women to open them to the Gospel. We couldn't do it. We had to have the supernatural.

It began to happen. To our delight, we started seeing souls saved, but sadly, people had been indoctrinated against speaking in tongues. Some were even taught it was of the devil. We patiently guided them through scripture, encouraging them to study their Bible and see what God had to say about it.

One such woman who had the unfortunate experience of this doctrine hosted a women's Bible study I was leading. She had been diligently studying the booklet I had given her. As the crowd was thinning out, she looked at me and said, "I'm ready. I am ready to receive my prayer language!" A few friends and I gathered around her, excitedly laid hands on her, and she began to speak with other tongues. She was blown away as she was filled with the Spirit, and she burst forth in joy. She was the first local person to get baptized in the Holy Ghost. After that, it started breaking out. The new converts started getting filled in the Spirit, and we began teaching about this walk of the Spirit.

One young lady showed up to our mid-week service on a Wednesday night. Some of the people attending the small church had witnessed to her. We were renting a small room on the third floor of a Nazarene church, and we had grown to 30 people. It doesn't sound like much, but because we slugged it out for every soul, we knew what victory this represented.

It was interesting observing her, wide-eyed, staring around the room as everything was different from what she grew up experiencing. The fact that we had keyboards, bass, and drums blew her mind. She listened to the sermon and responded to the call for salvation. She was weeping and had an encounter with God. I went up and introduced myself. She asked me if I wanted to hear her story. Surprised by her openness, I led her into the side room for some privacy. She poured her heart out. Her life was one of intense pain.

Her father had committed suicide, her mother had died of cancer, and she had inherited her three siblings while still a newlywed. I saw a young kid before me living under such intense weight. Her story continued: her husband had just left her with her best friend.

Moved with compassion, I could tell this young woman had every bit of hope destroyed.

A group of ladies was about to head out on a road trip to attend a women's conference, and I asked her if she would like to attend. She said, "Yes!"

We were headed from Philadelphia to the mountains of West Virginia. During a session, there was a call for the baptism of the Holy Ghost. She, too, had been taught it was of the devil. We told her Jesus said if you ask God for bread, He will not give you a serpent (Luke 11:11). This was a gift from a good Father, hers just for the asking.

She received and suddenly started speaking in tongues. She started weeping and praying. Then she started groaning in the Spirit (I'll share more on that later from Romans 8:26). She did not let up. The power and presence of God were all over her. The new believers looked at me and asked, "What do we do?"

I assured them, "God is doing a work in her. Healing, loving, soothing, and helping her."

We put her in a room and let God do what He needed to do. I told her, "Sweetheart, just stay in here and pray and weep, let God do whatever He needs to do." She stayed for several hours.

The Holy Spirit knows the adversity people face. He knows what breaks people and how to heal and restore them. Life had devastated this young woman repeatedly, victimizing her with abandonment. Yet, the Holy Spirit moved in and made her His habitation. He would never leave her (Hebrews 13:5).

This young woman would later tell me, "The night I went to church, I went to see if anyone cared; if not, I was going to go home and kill myself."

God intercepted her.

It was happening; the Holy Spirit was invading people, messing up their religious ideas, and showing them He was a person. He wasn't weird, but the One put in charge to lead and guide them in this life.

We began to see people filled with the Holy Spirit and speaking in tongues. We also received an offer from someone who said, "People like you—you guys are loving, you can use our building, just don't do the speaking in tongues thing ..."

My husband smiled and said, "No, thank you!"

Building a culture of praying in the Spirit happened by pattern, life by life as we discipled one soul at a time with laborers who knew personal and corporate victories of implementing this great tool provided by the Holy Spirit.

Although we were a small crew to start, we were setting the pace to praying in the Spirit. We took the Word literally as they did in the book of Acts. When someone was born again, we would soon demonstrate what it is to be filled with the Spirit with the evidence of speaking in tongues. We showed them in the Word how God wanted to give them a personal prayer language to help them be a bold witness and also to assist them in their walk of faith. The Holy Spirit is dedicated to seeing us walking in victory!

We held corporate prayer meetings in our homes. We would cry out in faith and pray in the Spirit, asking God to give us the strategy for our area. God knew how to reach the people and how to open wide their hearts to the things of heaven. We did not yield to excuses as we prayed weekly, contending for the Presence of the Holy Spirit. Young moms had their babies there, teaching by example that praying in tongues is normal. Those babies are now teenagers, and they know the sound of prayer.

We began to see a supernatural drawing of key people who would be the church's foundation. I challenged them to begin to pray in the Spirit as much as possible. Lives began to change. I would teach on the subject. One service, in particular, stands out to me. A man became agitated as I began to teach about the outpouring of the Holy Spirit. He finally just stood up and marched out in protest. He just didn't believe it, so he left the building. It wasn't too long until I noticed he was back again. We had dismissed the meeting, and people were chatting. He walked up to me and said, "I need to see your husband."

"Sure!" I said and directed him to Dave's office.

"I had to leave," he said. "I just didn't believe what she was teaching!" and with that, he stormed out. As he was driving down the road, right before him, there was a car accident in an intersection close to the church. He slammed on his brakes and suddenly started praying in the Holy Ghost! He was freaked out, but said that God told him to go back to the church, apologize and tell them, "Now, I believe." He then began to pray in the Spirit. I just grinned.

It is always best when the Holy Spirit does the convincing.

People began to be drawn, first for salvation, then baptism in water, and then baptism in the Holy Ghost. A Jewish woman was born again and believed in Jesus as her Messiah. We had a water baptism in the pool in our backyard. She was baptized the same day a woman who grew up in the Islamic religion got saved, and both started following Jesus. They were baptized in the Holy Spirit and faithfully started praying in tongues. Their life began to change drastically. Another woman involved in New Age ideology went to a women's book club at a friend's local coffee shop. She was on the verge of divorce. This woman responded to Jesus, gave her life to Him, and started attending our church. I knew she was hungry for spiritual truth; she was just in the wrong stream. I asked her if I could show her the right stream if she were interested. She was, so I did.

She renounced all the witchcraft, went through deliverance, and was filled with the Holy Ghost. She became an excellent student of the Spirit. She began to pray. Her husband got saved, the divorce was canceled, and now their family lives for God, and they are pillars in the ministry. All three of these women are currently in Bible School and hungry for God. I love when lives are intercepted by grace and mercy!

People from all over started praying in the Spirit. Unbeknownst to us, a woman who just loves praying in the Spirit would come to the church early in the morning, sit in her car, and just pray in tongues over the church. She had been doing it for a year before we realized this early morning intercessor was serious about her calling. A police officer even tapped on her car once because she was alone in a vehicle praying loudly. He asked if she was okay. She said, "Yes, officer, I am praying for my church, and I am praying over the police as well."

He was dumbfounded but thanked her. She continued steadfastly in prayer, and we gave her a key to the building. She faithfully gathered at the 4 am hour, and at the writing of this book, has prayed for seven years with others joining her. As a result, her testimony is wild. Her husband, who was lost in a deep, debilitating depression, snapped out of it after years and returned to his right mind. Her son and daughter-in-law came to Jesus, and her finances were blessed to the point she took an early retirement. But I watched this woman intercede in spite of all hell that came against her. The Holy Ghost had found a faithful prayer warrior, and He has gotten a lot of work done through her fervent and effective prayers. Only eternity will reveal what her prayers did in this region.

When you pray in the Holy Ghost and make it a part of not only your personal life but the corporate culture of the Church, it builds a team of Spirit-led people, setting them up for great and effective doors to open and for souls to be reached and rescued. How will they know unless there is a preacher? Someone must tell them, and it will take boldness to do it in this generation. The Gospel is the answer to every question—God alone has the power to change lives!

THE GOSPEL IS THE ANSWER TO EVERY QUESTION— GOD ALONE HAS THE POWER TO CHANGE LIVES!

We started in our living room with a dozen folks, and for a few years, we didn't have a building. We were the building, housing the presence of God. We shared Jesus with everyone anywhere, supermarkets, coffee shops, parking lots, and at the park. People started responding. It truly was supernatural. They were getting saved, healed, delivered, baptized in the ocean, filled with the Holy Ghost, and the radical thing ... they actually started praying! They started changing. They stayed with it, men, women, and some teens. When we pray in the Spirit, we change inwardly before change manifests outwardly. It is in this "change gap" where it is the easiest to decide not to continue praying. But when you have a culture of praying in the Spirit, you get carried past that place of wanting to quit. A praying church, regardless of the size, is a power to be reckoned with. This crew of praying folk would see many corporate victories. But as one who has had the privilege of watching this holy experiment, it has been glorious to see the transformation of the people from the inside. The outward victories have been supernatural, but the real wins were and are the lives that are changed.

It is my belief that everyone has souls connected to their life. We may have different administrations. For example, if someone's administration is to win a million souls for Jesus and another's administration is to win three, guess what? Each will be rewarded the same because both fulfilled their personal commission according to His glory in Christ Jesus.

God alone knows our assignment, our capacity, and our faithfulness, but we each have a part and a portion. God has given each of us an assignment. You need not compare your commission to anyone else's. All we have to do in life is the work He has given each of us to do. We will be rewarded accordingly. People ask me, "How can I know what I am supposed to do? What did God put me on the earth to do?"

I reply, "I am glad you asked," and I tell them about praying in the Holy Ghost. He has been given the charge to lead us through this life. When we pray in the Spirit, it builds us up past our sense-dominated walk where fear was and is our normal; but when praying in tongues becomes the new normal, He will cause us to walk out of those circumstances and into absolute victory.

GOD ALONE BRINGS BREAKTHROUGH

I don't know about you, but I have no clue how to get myself into my calling; I am simply not qualified to do so. But this I know, if I give myself to the Holy Ghost who according to Romans 8 knows the mind and counsel of God for my life, and if I'll be faithful to utter syllables regardless of what I feel, regardless of what it looks like, regardless that my mind does not understand it, if I will give myself to the Spirit of prayer, He will lead me there. If I let the Holy Spirit pray through me the perfect mind of God, He will bring me into divine appointment and destiny on purpose, on time, every time. I'm going to arrive where I'm supposed to arrive—on time, with character in place, bigger on the inside than on the outside.

> IF I LET THE HOLY SPIRIT PRAY THROUGH ME THE PERFECT MIND OF GOD, HE WILL BRING ME INTO DIVINE APPOINTMENT AND DESTINY ON PURPOSE, ON TIME, EVERY TIME

In truth, our heavenly assignment has had its challenges. I know in my own strength, I could not have done it. I would have quit. We were sent to a region that required a breakthrough, a breakthrough only God could bring. It required (and still requires) sacrifice, faithfulness, and faith in the promises of God.

I had heard some in the church-planting movement refer to the east coast as "the graveyard of Pentecostal preachers." I knew praying in the Spirit and uttering those mysteries before God was working a plan, even though it didn't look like it. I knew if God called us here, He wanted the treasure of the territory. Souls are the treasure.

It was God who equipped us to contend for a territory. Obedience to our assignment required putting our hand to the plow, sowing the seed, tending it, weeding the garden, watering, waiting … and waiting some more. There was a breakthrough beginning to happen. We gathered new believers and began to teach them about praying in the Spirit back then, and we do the same thing today. We would confess the promises God gave us as a church. We have possessed some of those promises that the Spirit went out ahead of us and prayed for. The Holy Spirit is our Helper and in charge of helping us walk out God's plan and purpose for our personal life and the life of a church.

I am humbled as I ponder all God has done in this area. I remember when there was no evidence of anything happening. I remember sitting in a prayer chair believing by faith that I would see what is a reality today. I remember when none of it existed. I also remember when it looked like I wasn't doing anything of significance yet, I was over in the spirit realm praying in tongues. It was work.

I had to decline some invitations to coffee or the movies. God needed a prayer partner. I was lifting weights in the spirit realm. The devil couldn't figure out what I was praying. In His wisdom, God does not allow the enemy to understand what we are praying.

The devil and his minions have no access. Satan cannot get in and mess it up. He has been left out of the equation when we pray in the Holy Ghost because it is perfect communion with the Spirit of God. Spirit-to-spirit communication. The enemy knows that if he is not successful in getting us out of prayer, the answer will manifest; it's going to come forth. The devil will hate what happens as God reveals His glory. The whole world is crying out for the answer. Where are those that would allow the Spirit to groan and pray through them? The earth groans, the Spirit groans, but does the Church groan? (Romans 8:26). The earth is groaning for the manifestations of the sons of God (Romans 8:19).

ACCESS TO GOD'S POWER

The lost are crying out for the answer. I submit unless we find the prayer closet and report to that prayer closet, giving ourselves to praying in the Holy Ghost, we will be limited to our best-laid plans and programs. There is a walk of power. One of the things that motivated me to pray in tongues was the fact that I was turning myself over to the One who had the authority and ability to transform me and make me a woman of God.

God is looking for a praying generation full of and controlled by the Holy Spirit, a generation that will not cower to culture but counter it with truth. His eyes are searching for a people who will stand with character, assured of their calling, a people tried and proven as the deep work of sanctification enables them to walk worthy of their calling. The Spirit does a work within us—we can only cooperate—it is His doing. He must transform us, so we carry the weight of His glory without it destroying us.

I want to be Holy Ghost made, not man-made. If I'm Holy Ghost made, I will not falter at either the accolades or the criticisms of people. Regardless of the persecution or the trial, find a prayer closet in the secret place [tongues]. Have the courage to do the spiritual work. What may seem like work in obscurity will become obvious. When we pray privately, it shows up publicly. Eventually, all the praying becomes evident.

When we give ourselves to tongues for edification, God builds our character, calling, and destiny. He will bring it forward on the appointed day for His praise, glory, and grace. You will look around and wonder how you stand where you stand. You will stand on bedrock. You will notice His presence with you. You will notice an anointing showing up around you.

Pray enough, and people will begin to ask, "What is the secret to the power?"

You'll tell them what the old-timers used to say, "Be much alone with Jesus." You will say to them, "Pray in the Spirit. Let God pray through you."

People have asked me, "How did you do it? How did you keep showing up and praying when you did not know what you were praying?"

My answer is this: "I was a woman desperate enough to start praying in tongues. I stumbled upon this truth by experience. The Holy Ghost has done this! I only showed up and prayed."

I love praying in the Spirit because it cancels out the enemy's plans for my life. Like many of you, he came after me at a young age. I know what a pit of depression looks like: despair, mental illness, generational curses, a spirit of suicide, a life not working, poverty, the frustration of not knowing how to make anything work when you have the potential. I didn't have a clue how to put it together. So, I just would report to the prayer closet [tongues], and I kept doing it day after day after day, year after year after year. And by year five, my life did not look the same.

Poverty broke off. The all too familiar cycles of failure, depression, and defeat were eradicated. I started winning. I vividly remember the day I prayed myself to a place of perfect peace. It was the first time in my life I felt that kind of peace.

There have been times when my soul was going through a storm so severe that I did not know how I would get up and preach, but there was my Helper, the Holy Ghost in it with me, moving in a way that brings glory to Jesus. During a storm, He carried me. I would go to my prayer room and weep before God. No one had a clue what I was going through because His peace was present, protecting me. The safest place in the storm is with Jesus. He is in the middle of the raging storm. My soul was growing more confident. I began to believe, "I'm going to make it through to the other side because I have a feeling that the Holy Ghost already prayed me through this."

As I mentioned, we live in a highly religious area, yet its people are very un-churched. We often share the Gospel with people who have no understanding of it. It is both refreshing and challenging. Most have not heard of a relationship with or the baptism of the Holy Spirit or praying in tongues. Yet we are seeing the Holy Spirit draw people. It is a divine setup.

The majority of our church is made up of first-time converts, so we have experienced the rest of this story in Acts as the Apostle Paul laid hands upon them, and they received the Holy Spirit and began to pray in tongues and prophesy (Acts 19:6).

I recall early on in our ministry when the Holy Spirit whispered to me a question: "Will you publicly pray in the Spirit? Will you demonstrate for them something they have not seen?"

Immediately I thought of all the questions I would get and all the "corrections" of those not understanding praying in the Spirit as a personal prayer language meant for personal edification—building rooms in my spirit that would house the revelation of God—and mistaking it for the specific gift of tongues which is intended to be followed by the interpretation of tongues when in a public assembly. (Note: I address the diversity of tongues in the Appendix.) I made a quick decision and told the Holy Ghost, "I am all in! I will do it! I will be a fool for Christ."

I am passionate about praying in tongues and allowing the Holy Spirit to have His way in a person's life, permanently transforming them. I love to teach disciples how to pray. To think we can pray and not ask amiss (James 4:3) astounds me. Praying in the Holy Ghost—praying in tongues—is foolproof if we'd only trust the Holy Ghost to pray through us. It only takes simple faith and trust.

CHAPTER NINE

BE FILLED

"The Spirit-filled life is not a special, deluxe edition of Christianity. It is part and parcel of the total plan of God for His people."

—A.W. TOZER

When we have received Jesus as our Savior, we are born into the family of God. Salvation is the trunk of the tree. The tree grows, and there are many branches. To say that if one does not speak in tongues they are not filled with the Spirit, would be an inaccurate statement. The Holy Spirit dwells within our born-again spirit. There is an indwelling; however, in scripture, we see an "infilling" as well.

> **INDWELLING:** *This happens because we get the Holy Ghost when we are saved. He is part of the Trinity—and the third person of the Godhead enters your heart at salvation.*
>
> **INFILLING:** *This is available to us after we are saved. If we choose to receive Him, we can be baptized in the Holy Spirit with the evidence of speaking in tongues. Tongues is the language of heaven. It is pure and undefiled. It is the language by which we communicate from our spirit to God's Spirit.*

The infilling of the Holy Spirit should not be a point of contention. Some have a mental stronghold that prevents them from receiving; however, scriptural truths and guidelines can help overcome any hindrance.

Some have been taught that praying in tongues is of the devil, that the gift ended with the death of the twelve apostles, or that it's only for uneducated or emotional people. I often wonder how this makes the Holy Spirit feel. After all, scripture declares that he who speaks in an unknown tongue speaks not to men but to God; in the Spirit, he speaks mysteries (1 Corinthians 14:2). Tongues is the communication of heaven. I have met others who feel they are not good enough to receive it—not worthy—and that it is only for chosen people. But God is not a respecter of persons (Romans 2:11).

A mental stronghold is a system of thought empowered by strong emotions. If one has been indoctrinated against praying in tongues, these thought patterns could block them from cooperating with God's truth. However, these types of fortresses can be pulled down by replacing them with God's Word (2 Corinthians 10:4).

Receiving the Holy Spirit is such an easy thing, but the devil tries to complicate it. It is a gift, a gift for all. Just as we received Jesus as our Lord and Savior by faith, we receive the Holy Spirit by faith.

The Holy Spirit has done a work of regeneration and is ready to fill you. God has done the work. It is our new, righteous nature, not our works, that God uses as the foundation for baptizing us in the Holy Spirit. The provision of the blood of Jesus makes us worthy to receive. We can *never* become good enough to *earn* the gift of the Holy Spirit or salvation. It is God's gift to give because HE is good.

When the Holy Spirit infills us, He wants to pray for us. He begins to create a supernatural language of tongues on the inside of our spirit. This language He creates in our spirit pours out and begins to form as language in our mouth. The moment we begin to give utterance to those syllables and start praying in tongues, we turn the Holy Spirit loose as our Teacher and Counselor. He comes into our life to edify, empower, teach, and sanctify.

I see the wisdom of the Holy Spirit in keeping our understanding out of our prayer language. When He begins to pray about our sins, we may abort the prayer, especially if it is a pet sin we justify. He goes to work to consecrate us and set us apart for His service. He edifies us past our problems, deals with our flesh and mental strongholds, all the while building us into a house that will bring Him glory.

In the book, *The Walk of the Spirit—The Walk of Power*, Dave Roberson skillfully explains:

> *There is a line drawn in the Spirit between the actual creation of the supernatural language in a believer's spirit and the journey of this language from his spirit to his lips to*

be uttered. It is on this line that the devil is most successful in erecting strongholds that hinder believers from speaking in tongues even after they have been filled with the Holy Spirit.

For example, many believers wrongly believe, for one reason or another, that God wants them to have the baptism in the Holy Spirit without the experience of speaking in tongues. Although this type of situation is possible, it is not the perfect will of God. People who think that way truly do not understand the great things God wants to accomplish in their lives through this simple but precious gift of speaking in tongues.

God has already provided the baptism. It is as simple as receiving it by faith and speaking it out. Some mistakenly think that God will just grab our mouth and make us start speaking. He will not. The Holy Spirit is a gentleman. He will not force us to do anything against our will. He is simply waiting for us to receive and give utterance to the beautiful, heavenly language He has already created in our born-again spirit. We see this truth displayed in Acts 2:4:

> "And they were all filled with the Holy Ghost, and began to speak with other tongues, as the Spirit gave them utterance" (KJV).

But the devil does his best to complicate what is rather simple. God is not reluctant to give this gift. He has already given it. The Spirit has already been poured out.

When one asks God to fill them with the Holy Spirit, they are filled. Some are filled with the Holy Spirit but have yet to speak in tongues. Many in this situation become discouraged. I tell them to speak the language by faith. Strongholds in the mind can block us from yielding over our tongue to the Spirit to utter the heavenly language.

Some are filled and struggle to pray with the few syllables they have received. I encourage them to continue to be faithful to pray daily in the Spirit, even if it is one or two syllables repeated over and over. I also encourage them to attend Holy Ghost prayer meetings, diligently study the scriptures, find a place of worship, and continue to surrender. When we worship, we prepare our souls to receive from God.

> **WHEN WE WORSHIP, WE PREPARE OUR SOULS TO RECEIVE FROM GOD**

Paul states:

> "And be not drunk with wine, wherein is excess; but be filled with the Spirit; Speaking to yourselves in psalms and hymns and spiritual songs, singing and making melody in your heart to the Lord."
>
> EPHESIANS 5:18-19, KJV

As you are in God's presence, begin to thank Him that it is already done, agree that you are a receiver of all His gifts. Thank Him for filling you with the Holy Spirit and for giving you the ability to speak in new tongues.

Our soul has the amazing ability to transform to what we most subject it. Jesus becomes to us whatever we worship Him as; Savior, Lord, Redeemer, Healer, Prosperity, Peace, and also Baptizer.

BENEFITS OF PRAYING IN TONGUES

There are many wonderful benefits of praying in tongues. Praying in the Holy Ghost:

- **Sanctifies us:** We cannot clean ourselves up. The Bible says that it is through the spirit that you mortify the deeds of the flesh (Romans 8:13).

- **Edifies us:** We build ourselves up in our faith. We get stronger and house the anointing of God (Jude 1:20).

- **Cleans our mouth up:** The Holy Ghost acts as a guardrail as our tongue stays subject to the Spirit. We cannot walk in victory and have a vicious mouth. Death and life are in the power of the tongue (Proverbs 18:21). We will eat the fruit of our words. Cursing, criticism, and careless confessions will crash our life. We have all had some mouth mishaps. James tells us that the tongue is most fierce. When we subject it to the Holy Spirit spending time praying in the Holy Ghost, we will begin to see our conversation come up higher.

- **Brings us peace:** Peace is another benefit to praying in tongues. We not only learn to walk in peace but we are also led by peace. The Holy Spirit guides us. When I am going in a direction, and my peace gets disturbed, I know He is warning me to stop, seek, and listen. I have learned not to move forward. I have also learned when He gives me the green light to progress with confidence.

- **Brings a refreshing:** "For with stammering lips and another tongue will he speak to His people. To whom he said, this is the rest wherewith ye may cause the weary to rest; and this is the refreshing: yet they would not hear" (Isaiah 28:11-12, KJV).

We all have those times where our schedule demands more of us than we have to give. I have found the practice of sitting in a chair and asking Holy Spirit to refresh me for one more task ahead; it doesn't take long. Sitting and praying ten minutes in the Spirit renews my strength and refreshes me as if I took a nap. It's supernatural.

- **Empowers us to be a witness:** The Holy Spirit gives us power and boldness to be a witness (Acts 1:8) and enables us to obey the great commission to "Go into all the world and preach the Gospel" (Mark 16:15-17, NIV).

The Holy Spirit gave me the power to be a witness for Jesus. Light shines best in dark places. He has given me the boldness to preach in the face of adversity. I recall a time I was on my way to a nail appointment. I got out of my car, and a woman was screaming. Her baby was choking. A crowd gathered. It was crazy! Something rose up in me, and I pointed at someone to please hold the woman. Two men were working on the baby, trying to get him to breathe. I knew why I was there. This was a 911 situation, and I know how to get a hold of God. I was right next to the men praying. The dad and another man were frantically trying to get the baby to breathe. I saw he was turning blue, and I didn't have time to care what anyone around me thought. I started praying out loud, "God, don't let this baby die!" I started praying in the Holy Ghost, not even fully aware, but we needed a miracle.

The police arrived, and they didn't wait for the ambulance as the hospital was so close. The baby made it there in time and was helped. It was the mercy of God. A few days later, it was in the newspaper. The father said, "All I know is I heard a woman praying, and she said, 'God, don't let this baby die!'"

I went back to where this couple lived. The mom answered the door, and I introduced myself. I began to share the Gospel with her. She responded and allowed me to pray for her. She asked me to come back because her boyfriend wanted to meet me. A few weeks later, I was headed to my nail appointment, and I saw him. I walked up and introduced myself, but he had already recognized me, and I was greeted with a big bear hug. He asked me to come upstairs to see the baby and his girlfriend. I began to share the Gospel with him. He told me something had happened to him that day. Every night when he would go to sleep, he heard a language inside of him. "It was how you were praying," he said. "Were you praying in sounds?"

"That was the Holy Spirit interceding for you and your little boy," I explained, and he was not afraid of it. He knew the only reason his son was alive was God's mercy. I prayed for them as I shared the Gospel. They both received Jesus. What gave me the boldness to enter the chaos with confidence? The Holy Spirit! That is the only answer. I am convinced that the couple would have buried their little baby had God in His mercy not intervened.

God is looking for people who will partner with Him who would know Him, be strong, and do exploits (Daniel 11:32). The Holy Spirit will give power to us to be a witness.

- **Brings us into Truth:** The Holy Spirit is the Spirit of Truth and inoculates us against deception. One of the signs of the end times is deception running rampant. We are living in that day. There are cultural wars that have their foundation in lies. As people of God, we need help to navigate the deception. The Holy Spirit operates like a vaccine, protecting us against deception. He is Truth and will not add Himself to a lie. The Holy Ghost leads us out of every lie and into the truth.

- **Reduces stress:** A study by the University of Pennsylvania took brain images of women as they spoke in tongues, or as the New York Post article said, "the rhythmic, language-like pattern that pours forth from religious people" (*A Neuroscientific Look at Speaking in Tongues*, November 7, 2006). The images showed that the thinking frontal lobe of their brains was quiet, while other parts of the brain that maintain self-consciousness were active.

  Other studies have shown physical benefits such as stress reduction by relaxing the mind, better sleep, and positive emotional management. There has even been a link to assisting the body's detoxification process because of the hormones released while praying in tongues (*10 Magnificent Health Benefits of Praying in Tongues for Mind and Spirit*, DrHealthBenefits.com, Scientific Review by Dr. Heben's Team). More on this will be included in the appendix.

IT'S TIME!

Perhaps you are ready to receive this wonderful gift of the Holy Spirit. Before you can receive the baptism of the Holy Spirit, your human spirit must be born again through Christ Jesus. You must receive a new nature that sets you free from sin.

Do you believe Jesus Christ is the Son of God and died for your sins, rose again, and wants to give you eternal life? If He is not your Savior, pray the following prayer from your heart:

> *Dear Jesus,*
>
> *Please come into my heart. I know I am a sinner. I believe You died for me and rose again. Please forgive my sins. I receive you as my Savior. I want to be born again.*

Welcome to the family of God!

If you are born again, the gift of the Holy Spirit is for you. It is only a matter of receiving this glorious gift. All you have to do is just ask in faith for the Lord to fill you with the Holy Spirit and give you the gift of speaking in tongues.

Now, focus on God and His faithfulness. Enter that place of worship where your mind and emotions are baptized in the presence of God; it is there the Holy Spirit will come upon you and flood your spirit. Praying in tongues is not emotional, but you may feel emotions, which is okay. It is His baptism.

When you pray, the Holy Spirit will come upon you. He will begin to move in your new nature, creating language inside your spirit. Your mouth and lips will have to form the language. He uses your voice which you activate by faith.

Pray this from your heart:

Heavenly Father,

You said in Your Word that You would give the Holy Spirit to those who ask. So in Jesus' name, I ask You to fill me with the Holy Spirit with the evidence of speaking in tongues. I believe and receive it now. Amen.

Once you have prayed this, rather than speaking in your native tongue, yield yourself to the Holy Spirit and begin to speak out those words you don't understand. You may hear sounds in your mind but speak them aloud by faith. It may sound like gibberish—baby talk—or it may just be one or two words; that is okay, speak it out by faith. You may have a full, rich language come forth that sounds like a foreign tongue with many words. That's okay, too! As you continue to yield to the Holy Spirit and speak out loud whatever language He gives you, you will soon have a flood of words bursting forth from your spirit.

I encourage you to pray in your new language faithfully for at least fifteen minutes a day, as this practice will solidify you in this gift. You will grow from there. Rejoice as you have entered into a glorious walk of the Spirit. An amazing adventure awaits …

WHEN YOU ENTER THE GLORIOUS WALK IN THE SPIRIT, AN AMAZING ADVENTURE AWAITS YOU ...

CHAPTER TEN

THE PLACE CALLED "DONE"

"Faith in God and His Word that is acted upon will bring results every time."

KENNETH E. HAGIN

I have consistently prayed in the Spirit for 25 years and have experienced the faithfulness of God. It has all been a process. Had you told me the day that the prophet ripped my sunglasses from my face that my life would look as it does today, you would have described ... a dream. A dream I thought was possible for others, but not for me.

Life in the Spirit has been a process. Yet just as God's mercy is new every morning, so has my journey with the Holy Spirit been. It has been filled with adventure and joy, as well as a painful but powerful progression. The most treasured aspect of it all has been getting to know Him. My relationship with the Holy Spirit has developed and deepened through trial and error. I have learned through walking with Him what pleases Him and what grieves Him. I have discovered the delight of His personality. He always points me to Jesus, who always points me to the Father.

I have often been taken aback by the Holy Spirit's humility and patience. He does not drive; He leads. He does not force me to follow but instead beckons me to come. When I am stuck, He does not travel ahead and yell over His shoulder, "You're on your own, kid!" No, He comes to my aid to help me when and where I am grounded.

It is typically in those moments, when emotions are screaming and courage is tempted to turn to cowardice, that Holy Spirit whispers the promises of the Father to me. He reminds me of what He has heard the Father and Son say over me.

A PLACE OF PROCESS

When God gives us a promise, it causes faith to arise. He then takes us through a process. Every promise of God is yes and amen (2 Corinthians 1:20).

The process is what happens during the middle—that place in between yes and amen. It is there, in the messy middle, that we must remember the promise, and we must worship God in the place called "Done." When we understand the finished work of Jesus, we realize we have already received everything He has promised. We do this by faith.

God responds to us and sees us through the eyes of faith. He treats us as if we have already "made it." He knows the 1,000 times we resisted, not just the one time we gave in. He believes with and for us. Our faith carries us over to the victory. That is why we can count it all joy when we fall into various trials because we have already won—regardless of the circumstances mocking the promise.

> "When all kinds of trials and temptations crowd into your lives, my brothers, don't resent them as intruders, but welcome them as friends! Realize that they come to test your faith and to produce in you the quality of endurance. But let the process go on until that endurance is fully developed, and you will find that you have become men of mature character with the right sort of independence."
>
> JAMES 1:2-4, JB PHILLIPS

In the place called Done, where your faith grasps the promise, joy emerges. You have it before you have it, so to speak. It is by faith that you receive the promises of God and experience victory before it shows up in the natural—in the place called Done. When you are in that place of faith, it is like you enjoy it (whatever it is that you're believing for) before you ever get it. You know it's yours even when nothing looks like it is yours. That is the place I throw my hands up in the air and worship God in the place called Done.

I worshipped in the place called Done when I needed healing in my emotions, from my past, in my finances, in my relationships, in my health, in my ministry, in my family, and for lost loved ones. I worship God because, in the finished work of Jesus, it has all been completed. I worship in faith as if I already possess what I am believing for. The Holy Spirit helps me to receive the promises of God in the here and now.

I admit that I am inclined to rush through the process. I don't really like process. I don't like working through and waiting through the process of deep healing, character refinement, skill development, or even rest and recovery. I want to get straight to the destination. I want immediate relief. Immediate release. Immediate resolution. Immediate victory. But I have discovered that more is accomplished in the process of becoming than when I actually receive the promise. Process is holy when we yield.

A PLACE OF CONFIDENT STRENGTH

When I embark on a battle, and as I continue to pray in the Spirit, I see the wisdom gained from the previous fights. Each skirmish has only made me stronger as the Holy Spirit used circumstances to produce character and develop maturity. We are constantly growing, but we rejoice that He will finish the work (Philippians 1:6). Our confidence is not in ourselves, in our own strength, but in Him. He will complete the work and keep us from falling (Jude 1:24), so we can throw our hands up in the air and praise Him as if we have already crossed the finish line bringing glory to Jesus.

I love that Paul declares this:

> "I feel sure that the One who has begun His good work in you will go on developing it until the day of Jesus Christ."
>
> PHILIPPIANS 1:6, JB PHILLIPS

When our faith goes out in worship to where it is finished—in that place called Done—confidence soars.

A PLACE OF VICTORY

Even in the midst of great and painful struggles, we are strengthened to endure harsh words and hard experiences as we have a lasting treasure in heaven. As the writer of Hebrews encourages us, we do not throw away our trust as it carries with it a rich reward in the world to come. We maintain our faith, even during trying times. We must remember, we are not left to ourselves. We are never alone, forsaken, or forgotten. Recognize what He did so you can operate in what He's done.

God is working in us something glorious. Faith is putting full confidence in the things we hope for; it means being certain of things we cannot see. It is this kind of faith that worships in the place called Done and pulls the promise from the unseen world into the seen world.

A PLACE OF DESTINY

I believe in the destiny God has planned for my life. If all my days are written in a book before I lived even one of them (Psalm 139:16), and He prearranged my days (Ephesians 2:10), then I can worship, live, and pray from the place called Done. You and I live from the finished work of Christ. This is salvation in action.

Let's take a closer look at the scripture.

> Your eyes saw my substance, being yet unformed. And in Your book they all were written, the days fashioned for me, when *as yet there* were none of them."
>
> PSALM 139:16-18, KJV

All my days ordained for me were written in His book before even one of them came to be. The plan for my life has already been written. I am not left alone to navigate the journey; I have been given a Traveling Companion who was there when it was written. Who better to take the lead in my life than the Holy Spirit? Remember, He transmits and discloses to me what He hears from the Father and Jesus.

Ephesians 2:10 states:

> "For we are God's [own] handiwork (His workmanship), recreated in Christ Jesus, [born anew}]that we may do those good works which God predestined (planned beforehand) for us [taking paths which He prepared ahead of time], that we should walk in them [living the good life which He prearranged and made ready for us to live]" (AMPC).

This passage speaks of the place called Done. It has already happened. We simply show up and do the praying to walk into all Jesus died to give us. Holy Spirit is guiding us the whole way.

I invite you to step into the place called Done—the place where you stand in the finished work, the already accomplished, where the future intersects with the present, and the glory and will of God are made manifest. You can stand in this place called Done by faith and learn to worship, pray, and praise from this posture.

> **STEP INTO THE PLACE CALLED DONE AND STAND IN THE FINISHED WORK**

The place called Done is a place of victory, peace, and provision. It is the place of overcome. It is a place where you stand in the completed promise and have the strength to push through everything that is a contradiction of circumstances between you and the fulfilled promise.

A PLACE OF ETERNAL HOPE

I have also experienced a place in intercession where faith goes out and believes for the lost to be saved. I do not believe there is a lost cause. I have seen people who were written off come in, respond to salvation, and get a hold of this message of praying in tongues. As they faithfully prayed, they began to transform. Through the process, real change occurred. They did not remain the same. This faith and these results are also the reason I refuse to give up on people. I know if I could persuade them to put their hand in the hand of the Holy Ghost and let Him pray through them, for them, their whole life would be intercepted by mercy.

I have also seen God's mercy bring salvation on death beds as well as others getting born again days before an untimely death. Again, I believe worshipping in the place called Done for souls to be saved is just as vital as worshipping for our needs to be met.

I have often prayed regarding our ministry, "Father, when people are done, when they can't go on, bring them on by here, intercept their lives, let them get saved, give them one more shot, help me to teach them to pray in the Spirit."

> "But you, beloved, building yourselves up in your most holy faith and praying in the Holy Spirit, keep yourselves in the love of God, waiting for the mercy of our Lord Jesus Christ that leads to eternal life. And have mercy on those who doubt; save others by snatching them out of the fire; to others show mercy with fear, hating even the garment stained by the flesh."
>
> JUDE 1:20-23, ESV

A PLACE OF REVEALED MYSTERIES

In his book, *In Plain View*, Robert Engelhardt writes, "The rightly balanced use of the gift of tongues is destined to recreate lives, peoples, and cultures for God's glory." I have witnessed Holy Spirit do this on a regular basis. Praying in tongues is a revelation gift. It will illuminate scripture; it will reveal all the people we are destined to meet, minister to, and help. Only the wisdom of God would hide this gift in a language spoken but not understood. He left our intellect out on purpose, and ironically, this is why many miss out. It is a gift of grace, and it takes faith to pray in tongues and to stand on promises and worship in the place called Done. Everything God has prepared for us is available to us.

Paul writes:

> "My message and my preaching were not with wise and persuasive words, but with a demonstration of the Spirit's power, so that your faith might not rest on human wisdom, but on God's power. We do, however, speak a message of wisdom among the mature, but not the wisdom of this age or of the rulers of this age, who are coming to nothing. No, we declare God's wisdom, a **mystery** that has been hidden and that God destined for our glory before time began. None of the rulers of this age understood it, for if they had, they would not have crucified the Lord of glory. However, as it is written: 'What no eye has seen, what no ear has heard, and what no human mind has conceived'—the things God has prepared for those who love Him—these are the things God has revealed to us by His Spirit. The Spirit searches all things, even the deep things of God."
>
> 1 CORINTHIANS 2:4-10, NIV (EMPHASIS ADDED)

When we pray in tongues, it is as though we construct rooms in our spirit that will house the revelation of God. A life in the Spirit abounds in revelation. The Holy Spirit guides us into all truth (John 16:13). He will teach us all things (John 14:26)—revelation of everything we need to prosper in our relationships, health, finances, careers … access to the mysteries of God as we commune with the Spirit and allow Him to breathe revelation into our spirit.

A PLACE OF ACCESS

I want to introduce people to the Holy Spirit. It is why I decided to write this book in the hope of getting this message out. As people, we are limited, but Holy Spirit is not. Everything is subject to prayer. When something is stubborn and won't move, stay in there and pray. It will turn.

The Holy Ghost is so vast. In this book, I am highlighting only the gift of praying in tongues as a personal prayer language. I know what it has done for me, and I am confident of what it will do for you.

Praying in the Spirit is not just an event that happens only once, so you can say you have been filled. Praying in the Spirit is to be engaged in as often as you desire. I believe when we pray in tongues, we are being transformed, and God prepares us to receive His promises. When we come upon the answers to our prayers, we will be equipped. Oftentimes, we pray for things God knows our character cannot handle. Rather than denying our request, our God of faith goes to work to prepare us to walk into what we have asked Him for. This process of preparation is a place where we could be tempted to think He is not answering our prayer rather than realizing, He indeed is. He is making us ready for the promise.

Standing in the place called Done and praying in the Holy Ghost is a practical way to access heaven and stand in positional truths before we have experienced them in the natural.

Start there and pray until you are aligned with those truths so completely—spirit, soul, and body—that the positional truth becomes your experienced reality. Say, "I am the righteousness of God in Christ …" Your confession must be walked out until it becomes your possession. It is not enough to say it; you must want it to be a manifested reality in your daily life.

Leave the place called Was and enter the place called Done.

A PLACE OF SAFETY

By building ourselves up on our most holy faith by praying in the Holy Ghost, we keep ourselves in the love of God (Jude 1:20-21). We receive His love for us and experience His love through us. We receive the Father's love by faith. Jude specifically speaks of how praying in the Spirit keeps us in the love of God. There is no safer place to be.

As I worship and pray from the place called Done, I often meditate on this scripture. There is such confidence in the One who keeps us.

> "Now to Him who is able to keep you from falling and to present you before His glory without fault and with unspeakable joy, to the only God, our Savior, be glory and majesty, power and authority, through Jesus Christ our Lord, before time was, now, and in all ages to come, amen."
>
> JUDE 1:24, JB PHILLIPS

CHAPTER ELEVEN

CLUB P.I.T.

"The plain unvarnished truth is, that every one of us
needs the accountability that comes from formal, regular,
intimate relationships with other godly people."

—WAYNE MACK

I am going to give you a challenge to pray. I believe we are all better with accountability. I have a group of friends who have committed to praying in the Spirit daily. In fact, we just finished a challenge to pray in tongues for an hour a day for one year. We simply put a checkmark daily once the praying was complete. It takes dedication to pray daily. It is also helpful when we have others doing it with us.

When you go to a gym, you are much more likely to show up regularly if you know a friend will be there waiting to meet and exercise with you. If you are going there alone and it is inconvenient, or you are tired or having an off day, you are much more likely to skip it, regardless of how healthy a habit or dedicated you are. Doing life together is better. Accountability is you reminding me of what I said I wanted to do.

> "If one falls, the other can help his friend get up. But how tragic it is for the one who is all alone when he falls. There is no one to help him get up."
> ECCLESIASTES 4:10, GW

Our goal of praying daily and using a checkmark the group can see for accountability are tools in place to serve us. We are not serving it. Life in the Spirit and praying in tongues is *never* about checking off a box or performing a religious ritual by rote. It is not self-help. It is not achievement. Within our group of friends who have made the commitment to pray in tongues an hour each day, there is great grace. When one of us misses this, for whatever reason, accountability is there for *encouragement*—never condemnation or punishment.

Wise Solomon knew that we do better together than we do alone:

> "Again, if two people lie down together, they can keep warm, but how can one person keep warm? Though one person may be overpowered by another, two people can resist one opponent. A triple-braided rope is not easily broken."
> ECCLESIASTES 4:11-12, GW

I like to think of the "triple-braided" rope as what happens when I have a covenant friendship—a strand of me, a strand of my friend, a strand of the Holy Spirit. There is a great deal of strength in the interweaving of our lives together with God and others.

WHAT IS CLUB P.I.T.?

P.I.T. is an acronym for Praying In Tongues because P.I.T. (Praying In Tongues) will keep you out of the PIT—the pit of depression, despair, failure, hurt, strife, unforgiveness, anger, poverty, pride, lust, control, manipulation, gossip, and a thousand other pitfalls the enemy of our soul has planned.

When we pray in tongues, the Holy Ghost goes out ahead of us on our path and navigates us around the traps, tricks, and trappings of the one who hunts our soul. He will redirect us around the plots and assignments of the enemy. He is there to lead and guide us, and He has no fear. We have been entrusted to Him. I liken the Holy Spirit to the Special Forces of heaven. He is making sure we get out of here in victory and with all the promises of God.

Keep in mind, it is the Spirit that does the work. We simply pray. We must be intentional about showing up. As the saying goes, "No one can do your push-ups for you." Only you can do the praying, but having others walk beside you on your prayer journey helps. Over the years, I would check in with people to see if they were still faithfully praying to provide encouragement. It began to grow. People began to share their experiences, and it served as a source of hope and help. Club P.I.T. was born.

As you are reading this book, I hope you are growing excited at the possibility of what your life would look like praying in the Spirit.

Perhaps a group where you can share your experience is something you are interested in. I invite you to join. You do not need to pray an hour a day to qualify. This is not a legalistic requirement; an hour is simply a metric. The point is to start praying and commit to regularly praying in the Spirit. The Holy Ghost will guide you.

JOIN CLUB P.I.T.

You can easily find us on Facebook under Club P.I.T. We are a community of Spirit-filled believers who encourage one another to pray in the Spirit. We share what He shows us, and we are a safe community to share these testimonies.

CLUB P.I.T. STORIES

Following are a few stories of people who have prayed in tongues to where their lives began to change. These are their testimonies in their own words.

As a pastor's kid, I grew up hearing many nuggets of wisdom, including the adage, "praying for an hour in tongues a day will change your life." This was wisdom I had head knowledge of but never put into practice. That is until February of 2020. I was driving home from a powerful conference with a friend. We excitedly talked about the work God did in us. Out of nowhere, I challenged us both to pray for an hour a day in tongues. We would hold each other accountable by simply texting prayer hands and a checkmark when we were done, and the other would love the message to confirm it was seen. Simple enough.

Little did I know how merciful the Lord was in His timing. We all know the hardship the year 2020 brought to the entire world. I know that my saving grace was praying for an hour in tongues a day. Some days I fought oppression and depression at a level I'd never experienced before. So I would lay in my bed scrolling social media, all the while making sure I was praying in tongues. It was all I had to give at the time.

Before I knew it, shackles began to fall off. Shackles I had lived with so long that I didn't notice they were gone until I realized my thought life had changed. My desires started to change. Decade-long patterns like binge eating and slothfulness suddenly didn't have the grasp they once did. I finally had the internal ability to say, "No!" I started to choose better.

It wasn't long before I couldn't live without my daily hour in tongues. On days I missed, I saw a marked decline in my attitude, behavior, and ability to choose a better way of living. Praying for an hour in tongues is now an essential daily practice I can not live without. And the best part is that I no longer have condemnation attached to everyday life. Whether I accomplish much or little, I am secure in my salvation and value in God. The Holy Spirit has worked so many issues and defaults out of my life by this simple practice and obedience to His leading. I've learned to humble myself and apologize for major and minor infractions, with my pride taking a backseat and embracing the cleansing flow of forgiveness and grace from my heavenly Father and those I'm in relationship with. I have a new desire to read and study God's Word, not out of duty but to know Him more.

I cannot encourage others enough to implement this practice in their lives. The change within is undeniable and has empowered me to live the Christian life in a way I never knew before!

—Hannah J.

Since I joined Club P.I.T., I have prayed in tongues each day for the past few years. I have experienced deliverance from strong temptations to return to past sins. Desires that would gnaw at my mind, I noticed after time, they just disappeared. Fear so strong that I was not about to face, but rather chose to run from and avoid, Holy Spirit completely obliterated.

Holy Spirit has been doing a work of increasing transparency and freedom in my life. Shining light in the darkness, having me reveal hidden secrets I've kept from family members and sharing stories of my past to others.

He also gave me the idea to house ministry students, becoming their live-in mentor, and He orchestrated the real estate transaction to make it a reality. I have experienced results of prayers I wouldn't have conceived to pray in my own intellect. The knowledge that whatever I'm praying, when praying in the Spirit, is the most effective thing I could be praying in the moment gives me the hope to continue the discipline.

—Crystal E.

For the past two years, I have been praying in tongues for at least one hour every day. Some days, it has been a challenge, but it has become second nature. I usually start to pray before I even get out of bed in the morning. I have had beautiful times with the Lord during my time of prayer in this season, but it has certainly not been all rainbows and sunshine.

Spending time with the Lord in this way gives Him access to the deep places within you. He can talk to you like a son or a daughter, instead of an orphan or slave. For someone who has had much trouble with the concept of being God's child, I can say that this can be very *uncomfortable*. I have been more uncomfortable in these past two years than I have ever been in my life. I have been more frustrated with myself than I have ever been in my life. A father does not talk to his children the same way he talks to other kids. His children have a relationship with him. He is able to correct, redirect, and encourage in a way that no one else can. This process of becoming a son or daughter can be awkward or painful, like someone throwing on a light in a room that only knows darkness. The initial reaction is to cover and hide, but the long-term outcome is better than we could ever imagine.

The God I have served all my life is becoming less of a distant figure from whom I am trying to win approval. With each passing day, I get a glimpse of the Father who knit me together in my mother's womb. I get a peek into the heart of the God who keeps count of how many hairs are on my head. It is still a fight, but I know that my Father will be patient with me. I have learned that if we do not quit, we cannot lose. If we only stay in the fight, we will be victorious. The God we serve has already won the victory. We fight evil knowing that, in the end, God wins. We know the end of the story before we even begin the battle. I cannot promise you constant comfort. I cannot promise that you will *feel* good all the time or that you'll even *feel* like praying. Serving God is not for the faint of heart. I can promise you that if you are willing to take this leap of faith and commit to praying in tongues regularly, the Lord will transform your life, whatever that means for you.

Praying in tongues has matured me in the Spirit faster than I ever imagined possible. When I look back at the girl who decided to begin praying in tongues for one hour every day, I don't even recognize her. I am so grateful that I made that decision, but I am hardly the same person. The more I pray, the more I understand how fully I need God. I used to think that maturity meant needing God less, but He is showing me that spiritual maturity means leaning on God **one hundred percent**. We never outgrow our need for God.

—Hannah M.

I would like to share a little bit of my story of how praying in tongues brings freedom. I had been Spirit-filled for a number of years yet did not walk in much victory. I love God, but I had so many bondages in my life. A particularly strong one was rejection. I live in the South, and at the time, Teresa and her husband were serving in a ministry there. She began to share with me how praying in tongues freed her from so many bondages. As she gave me testimonies and continued to share over a period of time, I began to see why the enemy had fought me so long to stay silent rather than pray in the Spirit. It is such a powerful gift that Jesus had given me!

I started praying and wouldn't stop. I saw the victory and freedom that Teresa had, and I wanted it. The Lord encouraged me to pray in tongues through her. Even when I didn't feel like doing it, I would press in; even when I stumbled, I would still pray. The strongholds began to weaken. As a little boy, I was violated repeatedly with sexual abuse. I was told I was a nobody and would not amount to anything. As a result, I searched for God in all the wrong places. I became a people pleaser and sinned against my own soul as I looked for love in all the wrong places. I was so confused about my sexuality. I needed healing.

As I continued praying in tongues, change started happening. I grew more secure. The Holy Spirit was healing my identity. I began to receive revelation that I was a child of God. I was not only accepted but adopted. I was chosen. I have walked in victory for many years now, and I am a confident man of God who worships God daily. If there is anything I would say about praying in tongues, it would be this: **don't quit**—even when your flesh screams at you to stop praying. If you continue, you will experience victory over hard taskmasters.

—Kevin R.

I was only 26 years old, and my life was a mess! I had lost everything—my parents, my marriage, my business, I was about to be homeless, and I was suicidal. I recommitted my life to Jesus, but something was still missing. I couldn't get past still wanting to take my life. That is *until I got baptized in the Holy Ghost.*

In all honesty, I was terrified of this "praying in tongues." You see, I came from a religious background that literally indoctrinated into me that tongues was a thing that passed away with the apostles in the Bible. I was taught that people who prayed in tongues in modern times were practicing a doctrine of demons. I was taught that "tongue talkers" have given themselves to be controlled by Satan. "Tongue talkers" were going to hell for sure! "Stay away, stay far away from those types of people!"

As I saw it demonstrated, I remembered my religious teachings and felt the fear wash over me that I would be sacrificed in the crowd of people displaying this "tongues" thing. Yet, I didn't care; as I still wanted to die, my life was so bad.

However, oddly enough, it was also the first time I felt peace in a life full of torment. I felt a heavenly presence so strong that I couldn't deny it was God. As I silenced my racing mind, I knew I felt God.

In a private moment, in the silence, I looked into the mirror, and I had a conversation with God and spoke the words I will never forget, "God, if this is of you, and it's a gift, a good gift, I want it! I need it; please God, show me." Immediately words of an unknown tongue came bursting out of my mouth. My heart was racing in fear and yet also in freedom!

That moment went into what seemed like a time warp of five hours of praying, weeping, and groaning in the Spirit—praying in tongues. I felt a safety, a loosening I can't explain. That day, that gift saved my life and enabled me to feel a freedom I had never felt.

Praying in tongues is normal and life-saving! I will never not believe or stop using my precious gift of tongues.

—Elaina C.

I grew up in a church culture that was anything but charismatic. We sang reverent hymns but never clapped during or applauded after a song, we didn't raise our hands in worship, and we most certainly did not pray in tongues. I was taught about the Holy Spirit, but my reference point of Him was that He was a silent partner in the Trinity; He didn't really do much for us in our daily lives.

I cringe at the thought of how much I missed not being in communion with the Holy Spirit, but fortunately, when I was 35 years old, I encountered the person of the Holy Spirit at a women's event, and everything in my life changed. A minister put her hand on my belly, and my mouth began to make a sound that I didn't understand or have control of, but I yielded. I yielded to the power that I felt flood me from the bottom of my feet to the very last hair at the top of my head.

After leaving that event, I didn't know how to use this new gift. I didn't realize I could employ it anytime, anywhere, and I could communicate with the Spirit of the living God in my everyday life.

Shortly after that event, two months to be exact, I found NDCC. Pastor Dave and Teresa Verdecchio discipled me and taught me the full Gospel and that a sign that would follow believers of Jesus Christ was the evidence of speaking in tongues. They gave me testimonies of their own life and biblical references where we are encouraged to pray in the Spirit and pray often.

One Sunday, Pastor Dave was preaching, and he said something that changed the trajectory of my life. He said that if I committed to praying in the Spirit for one hour a day, I would receive revelation, freedom, and healing, and my life would never be the same.

Challenge accepted.

He didn't know this about me, but I'm a very literal person. If you tell me to do "this" in order to obtain "that," I'll do it exactly as you say. So after church, I was determined to pray in the Spirit for an hour a day, which I did for the entire summer and beyond in 2018.

As I'm writing this, I don't have adequate words to describe the healing that came from my time in communion with the Holy Spirit. How that summer, there were motives, perspectives, beliefs, and paradigms that began to change in me from the inside out. That time of prayer, seeking, and devotion burned up in me; things that I didn't know were hurting me and keeping me from stepping into the calling God had on my life.

I encourage anyone that has received their prayer language to pray and pray often. It is one of the greatest weapons we have against the enemy, the greatest tool to bring heaven down to earth, and the sweetest exchange as you become best friends with the Holy Spirit. I thank Jesus daily for the gift of praying in tongues.

—Cynthia P.

As a young boy, I grew up in a house often hearing my mom pray in tongues. So, I would often mimic what I heard, not having a true understanding until I grew up. As a teen, I was a very angry, withdrawn young man. I didn't discover how praying in tongues could change my life until I was married and became a father. My oldest son would have trouble sleeping, and I was rediscovering my love for God at the time. So I would often rock him to sleep and take that time to pray in the Spirit. During that time, a lot of my own fear and doubts started to drop off. I would continue to do this before all my training assignments and missions while serving with my unit. If anything, just to give me peace of mind and bless us while we worked.

However, it wasn't until recently that I really experienced the power of praying in tongues. A lot of the hurts I experienced as a child, being sexually abused being the biggest, began to rise to the surface, complete with all its shame. This time, it was not present to torment me but so that Jesus could touch those places in me and heal them. I struggled with rejection and insecurity. I did not believe anyone liked who I really was. Many times I questioned my own manhood and felt like a failure. During my time in prayer and praying in tongues, God began to show me the truth and melt away my insecurities. He spoke to me about my identity as I learned what God said about me. He removed the shame and showed me things that happened to me as a child were not my fault. Praying in tongues has allowed me to have a deeper relationship with God, brought healing to many deep-seated wounds, and shaped me as a father and husband.

—Dallas D.

As a young man living in Paris as part of a mission organization planting churches in hard territory, I knew that there had to be more to my life. I was so hungry for God and desperate for His power and presence in my life. The missionaries I lived with told me about a woman from Philadelphia who advised them to "pray in tongues one hour a day." I started to pray. When I finally met Pastor Teresa Verdecchio, the revelation of praying in tongues was explained to me more fully. I began to pray without ceasing as I was suddenly gripped by this intense desire to pray so that I might know Jesus more.

One day I came home from work in the afternoon. I decided to pray for a solid hour in tongues. As I prayed, power began to manifest on my physical body, and I felt currents of electricity pulsing through me. Throughout my day, I would go to the store and get words of knowledge for people. The prophetic gift started to flow more seamlessly. A man came into the store I was working at soon after I began to pray for long hours in tongues. All of a sudden, I heard the Spirit say, "Arthritis. Back pain." During my conversation with him, I asked if this was true. He was in shock. I prayed for him, and he felt tremendous heat in his lower back and said the pain was gone!

As I continued to pray the syllables of victory, my life began to change radically. I started to get freedom in my oppressed mind, healing in my broken emotions, and the Lord began leading and guiding me as I prayed out the will of God for my life. Dreams and revelation started to come with greater clarity. I am a deeply transformed and blessed man as a result!

—Doug K.

It wasn't until I started praying in tongues with intentionality that things began to change *for* me and *in* me. At the suggestion of my pastors, I started praying in tongues for longer periods of time than I had been used to. And miraculously, things began to be different.

A few years ago, my pastor knelt down next to me as I was praying, and she prophesied that wisdom and revelation would explode in me. I believe I am seeing that prophecy fulfilled as I started praying in tongues each day.

I have found that praying in tongues is not an exercise in futility but one that allows the Lord to accomplish great things in my life. One area of transformation was deliverance from strongholds of a sexual vice I had tried to conquer in my own strength for years (and failed miserably). This stronghold was demolished through praying in tongues in a relatively short amount of time.

Gossip, backbiting, and even my hard-heartedness also have crumbled and are now lying at my feet. As I watch that dust settle, my faith is being built up each time I meet with God in this way. So much has changed as I began speaking to Him in this most intimate language. It is my most favorite love language.

The scripture that comes to mind immediately is, "But ye, beloved, building yourself up on your most Holy Faith, praying in Holy Ghost" (Jude 1:20, KJV).

—Flo Z.

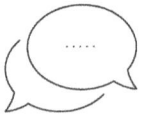

When I was filled with the Holy Spirit, I really didn't understand what was going on. After a friend of mine got filled with the Holy Spirit, a man at the prayer meeting told me it was my turn. As they were praying over me to receive my prayer language, I thought, *this is stupid; this isn't real!* But I knew that was the enemy's lies. I pushed past the lies and allowed the Holy Spirit to flow. I started out with babbles—just a few syllables. It didn't sound like much, but I practiced my prayer language every day to strengthen and develop it.

There are times when I feel I need to pray, but I have no idea what to say, so I pray in tongues. It's pretty awesome because I can be thinking about a person or situation in my mind and pray in the Spirit over that. I know that God's perfect will is being prayed for. Being filled with the Holy Spirit is another connection to heaven and avenue to hear from God. The Holy Spirit has empowered me to do the will of God and call heaven down to earth. I couldn't imagine life any different.

—Tina S.

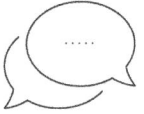

I was 19 years old and a freshman in college when I met a group of students on fire for Jesus. I joined them in different dorm rooms every night as we prayed for people to be filled with the Holy Spirit. I was so hungry for God and in need of His power in my life that I was determined to get it too. One night, after sitting out in the winter cold crying out to God, I returned to my dorm. One of the girls who was baptized in the Holy Spirit the night before said to me, "Maybe you need to just worship God anyway."

I nearly bit her head off and went to my room. After repenting for my attitude, I agreed and began to worship God and pour my love on Him, right there in my bed. I raised my hands as I worshipped, and the next thing I knew, the words coming out of my mouth were not English. I was ecstatic at my new gift of the Holy Spirit and began praying in tongues everywhere. I was quickly met with great opposition, especially when I went home to my local church that weekend. They taught in our class that speaking in tongues was not for today. I could not deny what happened to me but needed biblical answers I did not have at that point in my life. I began to dig everywhere in the Bible for verses on the Holy Spirit and speaking in tongues.

About two months later, while at college, I went to a Thursday service right before Easter. I had a vision of Jesus on the cross, and He told me how He had to die for me so that I could live, then I saw Him before He ascended into heaven. I was pleading with Jesus not to leave me. He said He had to go so He could send the Holy Spirit. At that moment, I began to pray in tongues and knew that it was real. He did send the Holy Spirit, and I now have Him too.

Soon after that, I had a word of knowledge while praying in tongues on campus. I kept praying and asking the Holy Spirit where to go. He led me to a student experiencing the same pain that I was. I knew then it was God that led me there to pray for her healing. I was so hungry for God. I spent the next 32 years pursuing more, never fully realizing that I already had everything I needed. More than seven years ago, I came to New Destiny Christian Center.

It was the first time I could pray in tongues with freedom, and the call on my life as an intercessor was not only acknowledged but encouraged. The more I prayed in tongues, the more I began to see in the spirit realm. With the visions came words of knowledge. Sometimes body parts would be highlighted to me; then, I would pray out healing over them in English.

On December 14, 2014, a prophetic word was spoken over me by my Pastor, Teresa Verdecchio. She said, "Because you are such a prayer warrior, you will also be a person of faith. You will speak things into being that God shows you. And not only you but your husband and son will be with you. As for me and my house, we will serve the Lord."

Little did she or I know at that time that four years later, my life would be turned upside down and that my husband and I would face the greatest battle of our lives and marriage. In 2018, my husband became crippled with anxiety and depression. He was unable to leave our home to go to his job or even see his own mother, who lived nearby our home. After a year, we feared that he would not even be able to attend our son's wedding. With less than six weeks to go, his hair was past his shoulders and his beard to his chest. But I refused to accept anything other than what God had promised me, and I continued in daily prayer, "taking care of God's house," believing God would take care of mine.

For months, I would read *Declarations and Decrees*, a mini-book by Teresa Verdecchio, over my husband. He began to read them out loud over himself. We read books on deliverance and would stand and worship in our living room by faith. Every opportunity I had, going to and from work, even on the job, I prayed in tongues.

Not only was it building me up in my faith, but the visions increased. I saw my husband with me in church, on the platform, playing guitar, following him out of the building … I know that strongholds were being torn down in both our lives. God showed me that He alone is my strength and my fortress, that my security needed to be in Christ alone.

I encountered God daily and penned poems that came from time spent with God and praying in the Holy Spirit to release them in English. I should have fallen apart, but rather was given strength and hope from the Holy Spirit to see the day my husband would be free and that God would use us to help set others free.

Now, not only do my husband and I read the Word of God daily, we attend our church together faithfully. We also serve together joyfully in our children's ministry. In 2021, my husband, son, and I were all baptized. In that same service, my son and his wife gave their lives to Jesus and have begun attending church with us. Recently, my son was baptized in the Holy Spirit and spoke in tongues too! (And yes, my husband made the wedding, and it was a beautiful celebration!)

Our pastor has often said, "Pray in tongues an hour a day, and in five years, you will not recognize yourself." Praying in tongues has not only changed my life by a deeper, more intimate walk with God, but through it, God has saved my husband's life and saved our marriage. My future has completely changed by praying in tongues, and God has given me a new destiny. The Holy Spirit has taken me places I never imagined, and I can't wait to see what He has in store for our future.

—Mary Beth J.

The trajectory of my life and destiny has completely changed since being challenged 19 years ago by Pastor Teresa Verdecchio to pray in tongues daily. I received the Holy Spirit and first spoke in tongues as a young child, but after that, I did not engage in praying in tongues again until my mid-twenties when meeting and getting to know Pastor Teresa and hearing her speak about the power behind praying in tongues. I wasn't even sure if I still could, but I opened my mouth by faith, and instantly my heavenly language was there. It was as if I had been using it since I first received it.

Since that time, God has amazed me by taking me from a small southern town to traveling the world sharing the love of Jesus, revealing to me musical talent within that I never knew existed and so many other provisions, protections, and personal deliverances. Praying in tongues, enlisting the help of the Holy Spirit, and using this gift from our heavenly Father is imperative in experiencing the power of the kingdom on earth and in our daily lives!

—Jeanette D.

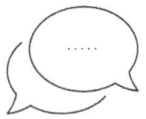

I believe praying in tongues was a helpful tool God used to rewrite my destiny with His pen of mercy. I received the Holy Spirit as a teen but never tapped into its fullness until I met Pastor Teresa ten years ago. She taught me about the Holy Spirit and His power to transform as she challenged me to pray in the Spirit every day.

I did.

Since then, my life has completely shifted. I went from being a North Philadelphia young girl, a victim of poverty and abuse, depressed with no hope for the future, to a licensed social worker working in the community God rescued me out of. The power of the Holy Spirit and speaking in tongues revealed God's nature in me and gave me the power and tools I needed to change my life. I came to know Holy Spirit as Comforter, Helper, and Counselor.

—Lisa V.

I thank God for the gift of speaking in tongues. When I was a new Christian, I received the baptism of the Holy Spirit. I had no clue of the powerful effect it would have on my life and walk with Jesus. I remember not understanding what exactly praying in tongues meant, but I did what my pastor suggested—pray in tongues anyway! Pastor Teresa encouraged and challenged me to pray in tongues for one hour a day. That was five years ago, and my life radically changed as I remained faithful to pray.

During that challenge, the Lord gave me a vision, it was powerful, and it gave me understanding and clarity about praying in tongues. In the vision, I was on my knees praying in the Spirit. As I was praying, I saw a demon sitting next to me. The demon would leave immediately after I stopped praying in tongues but would instantly reappear every time I started praying in tongues. While I was in the vision and seeing this demon sitting next to me, I was afraid. It made me feel like I was doing something evil.

After I came out of the vision, the Holy Spirit revealed the truth in what I saw. The Lord revealed a strategy from hell, showing me that the devil doesn't want Christians praying in tongues. I realized that the enemy is afraid of Christians actively praying in tongues because of the power of this type of communication with God.

Praying in tongues has transformed my walk with Jesus. It has allowed me to pray the perfect will of my Father for my life. I have received inner healing, understanding, confidence, boldness, deliverance, healing in my sexuality, and new levels of freedom in Christ! If I didn't pray in tongues, I truly believe I would still struggle in many areas such as fear, shame, depression, condemnation, anger, and even sexual sin.

Praying in tongues is an amazing weapon that every Christian should use! My life is an example of what praying in tongues can do for you. I have been transformed from the inside out, all for His glory. Praying in tongues has not only set me free, but it has kept me free in many areas where I once struggled.

The Holy Spirit built me up in the things of God. Praying in the Spirit has sharpened my gifting in Christ and strengthened me on the inside to go into the hard places to share the Gospel with the lost and dying—including my son. I have become a bold witness and have led some of my family members to Jesus on their deathbed. My changed life convinced them of Jesus.

I thank God for the gift of praying in tongues. It truly does change how you think, speak, act, and react to the world around you.

For me, it has made my process in Christ a beautiful adventure of experiencing the Father's love and the plans that He desires for me to walk in. It is my prayer that everyone who reads this book will experience revelation about praying in tongues and be activated in this free gift.

—Tiffany A.

Growing up with different religious experiences, I was drawn to a particular sound and the supernatural. As a young girl, I went to revival services and heard people praying, but I did not understand what they said. I was just caught up in the miracles and healing, which piqued my curiosity.

In my adolescent years, I again remember witnessing a group of charismatic Catholics meeting in a house basement praying, and I was drawn to the "sound." I remember sitting at the top of the steps watching with anticipation at what would happen.

In 2006-2007, I began to struggle with the different teachings on whether praying in tongues was still for today. I searched out the arguments for different views and opinions and became confused and frustrated because I wanted a clear, definitive answer. I remember praying and asking the Holy Spirit to forgive me for not believing and grieving Him, but in faith, I would begin to pray with whatever syllables He gave me, and I would know the truth. When I first started praying in tongues, my prayer life went from mundane and powerless prayers to powerful prayers. I felt like I was plugged into a power source and could pray for hours. Although I had no understanding, I felt things being shifted and broken off. My desires and longings began to change. There were times that I would be on the floor groaning and crying, knowing that I was partnering with the Holy Spirit, interceding and standing in the gap for someone. I firmly believe that one of these encounters aborted the plan the enemy had set in place to have my son take his life.

Praying in tongues has changed my whole life! I pray with expectancy and anticipation, believing for the power promised to us in Acts 1:8, the same outpouring of the Holy Spirit in Acts 2, to empower us to take the Gospel to the lost and walk in signs, miracles, and wonders.

—Nancy G.

Praying in tongues has changed my life and walk. It has helped guide my family, business, and life. It has also broken generational curses and strongholds and supplied wisdom to make the right decisions in my finances. I'm thankful God has given me this gift that allows me to tap into supernatural guidance. Holy Spirit has helped me understand the call on my call in life. I am learning how to communicate with God in a practical way.

—Angel G.

Praying in tongues changed my life. I can remember having numerous conversations with my husband about his desire to pray in tongues. During that time, I truly did not understand it and did not think I needed it or that it was for everyone. After all, I grew up in church and could count on one hand the number of Christians I heard speak in tongues. But I wanted it badly for him because of how passionate he was about his need to speak in tongues.

After encountering the Holy Spirit in July 2018, I wanted everything God had for me. So when the teacher asked during my first Biblical Studies class in August that year if I wanted to receive the gift of the Holy Spirit, I emphatically said, "Yes!" That night I had such a vivid dream where God came to visit me, and life-changing things happened in that dream. I woke up praying in tongues and could hear God telling me whom to pray for and how. From that day, I began to pray in tongues all the time. I believe that is how chains of bondage were broken off of my life so rapidly.

I didn't know my true identity in Christ; I was so caught up in trying to be perfect, including my image of how people saw me, but God revealed to me that I am His masterpiece. I found myself trying to fill the Jesus-sized hole in my heart with addictive behaviors, including shopping, working out, and drinking every night. As I began to pray in tongues, He immediately removed my desire for alcohol! Three and a half years later, I have never craved or have been tempted by alcohol.

Today, three and a half years later, my husband is in awe of what God has done in my life in such a short time. He restored the years the locust has eaten, and I know that without a shadow of a doubt, it is from a Spirit-filled life of praying in tongues.

Praying in tongues liberates me, gives me peace, gives me guidance, gives me comfort, gives me boldness, gives me strength, and activates my spiritual gifts. And most importantly, it gives me a deeper relationship with God.

—Kia L.

APPENDIX

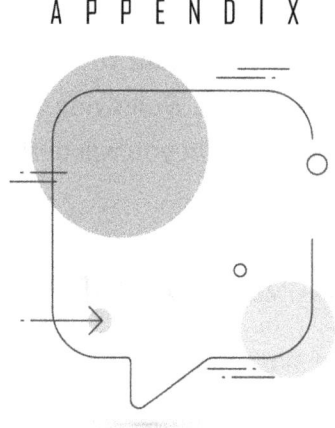

DIVERSITY OF TONGUES

"The gift of tongues, like all of God's blessings, should
be sought with a humble and faith-filled heart."

—ROBERT ENGELHARDT

Please note that the devoted focus of this book was on tongues for edification, which is also known as our personal prayer language. There are tremendous, exhaustive works on all the gifts of the Holy Spirit and how He operates with various gifts and administrations. I will list several of those in the back. I did not feel led to write that kind of work. I am called to encourage people to pray in the Spirit, and I hope to provide understanding as to what can happen when one consistently prays in tongues.

Though my focus was on the gift of tongues for the edification of the believer, I feel it is important to introduce the diversity of tongues given to us in scripture. Following is a brief description of each, and I hope as you read that you will desire to dive deeper and search out more.

UNDERSTANDING SPIRITUAL GIFTS

Just as the Holy Spirit has fruit (Galatians 5), He also has gifts. In 1 Corinthians 12:8-10, we see the nine gifts of the Spirit listed.

1. Word of wisdom
2. Word of knowledge
3. The gift of faith
4. Gifts of healing
5. Working of miracles
6. Prophesy
7. Discerning of spirits
8. **Divers tongues** (or different supernatural manifestations of tongues)
9. Interpretation and tongues

Not only do we get the fruit of the Holy Spirit, but we have also been given His gifts. I want to focus here briefly on divers tongues. The operation of praying in the Spirit cannot be understood with our intellect. It is crazy to think that I can pray in a language that neither I nor anyone else can understand and that it will deliver me into all God has purposed I would walk in. As foolish as it sounds, it is true.

What does the Bible mean when it says *divers*. Divers and diversity mean differences. "Divers tongues" or "diversity of tongues," tell us there are different flows or manifestations to speaking in tongues.

There is much confusion and division on this subject; I believe, in part, due to misunderstanding and applying the same set of rules to a different operation of tongues. There are four distinct operations or manifestations of tongues.

FOUR BASIC OPERATIONS OF TONGUES IN THE WORD

The Word of God outlines four basic operations for the gift of tongues. Here is a brief overview:

1. **Tongues as a sign for unbelievers** (1 Corinthians 14:22). This is what took place on the day of Pentecost (Acts 2:4-11). This happens when the Holy Spirit bypasses a believer's mind and speaks a language that they do not know or understand, enabling one to preach and bring glory to the name of Christ.

2. **Tongues and interpretation of tongues** (1 Corinthians 14:5). This operation of tongues is normally done in a public assembly of believers. Someone prays in tongues, and an interpretation comes forth from them or another person.

3. **Tongues for intercession** (Romans 8:26). This is where the Holy Spirit begins to take over the intercession as we stand in the gap and make up the hedge praying for others, ourselves, families, church, communities, cities, and nations.

This is where the Holy Spirit comes alongside us and prays for us, through us, and with us.

4. **Tongues for personal edification** (1 Corinthians 14:4; Jude 1:20). We receive this supernatural heavenly language when we are baptized in the Holy Ghost. We can pray as much and as often as we desire. We are not waiting on an unction as we can give utterance to tongues at any time when we are filled with the Spirit. Three of the four diversities of tongues are all given as the Spirit wills (1 Corinthians 12:28). But there is one diversity of tongues—for personal edification—that you can operate at will and pray as much as you want. We are the captain of this gift. The others are as the Spirit wills.

Different rules govern each of these operations. Two are designed to operate in the life of a believer:

- tongues for edification
- tongues for deep intercessional groanings of the Holy Ghost

Two are for the public assembly:

- tongues for interpretation
- tongues as signs for unbelievers

When someone walks into a Spirit-filled church, they may hear people singing or praying in the Spirit. They are not functioning in tongues and interpretation or as a sign to unbelievers. They are using their heavenly language, speaking to God, not to man. There is a misunderstanding of the diversities. It would clear up much if this simple distinction were understood. I do not believe the answer is to not speak in tongues in public so as not to confuse anyone. That is not biblical. We see examples of this use in scripture. The answer is to educate with humility about the various operations of tongues.

The prayer language we receive when we are baptized in the Holy Ghost is powerful. He knows what we are called to do in the earth. I do not know your calling. But I can encourage you to pray in the Holy Ghost as He knows your purpose. Our calling is hidden in seed form. "But unto every one of us is given grace according to the measure of the gift of Christ" (Ephesians 4:7, KJV).

It is a wonderful journey of discovery as we pray out the mysteries of God for our personal life. Praying in tongues is used by God to transfer divine mysteries from Him to us. We have been made the stewards of our own edification.

The Holy Ghost gives us the strength to do the things we cannot do on our own. Things like walking in love and forgiving when hurt, slandered or lied about are examples. We cannot do this in our own strength, but everything changes when the Spirit goes to work. We are able to do what we cannot. Holy Spirit builds strength into our spirit.

I want to share my personal experience with each diversity of tongues as they manifested through me.

1. TONGUES AS A SIGN FOR UNBELIEVERS

I was asked to meet with a missionary's wife. They were soon to leave the country. She had questions about being filled with the Holy Spirit and wished to inquire of me. Her husband was Spirit-filled, but she grew up in a denomination that did not believe it was for today.

I went to her house. We visited for a moment, and then she jumped in with her questions. I did my best to answer them, but I could tell she was still a bit unsure. I asked her if she wanted to pray to receive. I knew God would have to do something as her five children were running around the house, and she couldn't get a moment without an interruption. She said, "Yes, please pray!"

I asked Father to fill her with the baptism of the Holy Ghost in the name of Jesus and then started to pray in tongues. She immediately looked up at me and said, "You know Latin?"

To which I replied, "I do not!"

Her eyes grew big. She said, "You just said, 'Liberte corde eius.' In Latin, that means "Free her heart."

I watched her countenance change before my eyes. She looked at me and said excitedly, "I believe!" And at that moment, she received her heavenly prayer language.

The Holy Spirit gave her a sign.

On another occasion, I was ministering in a church in Philadelphia. During the altar call, the Holy Ghost came upon me strong, and I was led to pray in tongues. I did so for several minutes. He was moving, and I was obeying. Healings took place, salvation and deliverance, words of knowledge, and prophecy. The service was dismissed, and a young lady came up to me grinning. I greeted her as I was no stranger to this ministry. She hugged me and exclaimed, "I did not know you knew Spanish!"

I told her, "Sadly, I do not know Spanish. I wish I did."

"Well, you spoke in Spanish the whole time you were talking about Jesus," she said. "I was looking around in amazement at how fluent you were and then figured everyone must have known you speak Spanish."

I shook my head and told her, "That was the Holy Ghost. He was giving you a message. I do not speak Spanish. But He knows every language and how to speak to us, and He just spoke to you."

She was amazed. So was I!

2. TONGUES AND INTERPRETATION OF TONGUES

I have been in church my whole life and have seen this operation many times. Someone in the congregation prays in tongues, and another gives the interpretation. I have sensed the Holy Spirit give me the unction to speak out in tongues, and I have done that. I have also received the interpretation of tongues, and I spoke it out faithfully as I heard it.

From praying much in the Holy Spirit, I had learned to isolate the channel by which He speaks. So I was pleasantly surprised when someone spoke in tongues, and I could hear God so clearly. I remember as a little girl being in a service where God was moving, and I would hear the Holy Ghost praying on the inside of me. I did not realize then that it may have been this gift in operation. It is to be noted here that it is the same as prophecy when tongues and interpretation flow together.

3. TONGUES FOR INTERCESSION

There have been times when I didn't feel I could go on. One story was during a time I had been giving myself intentionally to a season of much prayer. I added some fasting to it. In my book *Crushing Condemnation*, I share some of my story of sexual abuse. As a result of numerous violations, I had a stronghold of uncleanness. It was a monster in the basement of my soul that I worked desperately to keep contained. But there were times when it would call my name.

One Friday night in Denver, it took everything in me to go to the weekly prayer meeting that I loved. But this night was different. I did not want to be there. I didn't like anyone or anything. My emotions were so antagonistic toward praying in the Spirit. I wanted the prayer leader to shut up. My mind was in a war. I wanted to run. I wanted to leave all of this and just go find trouble.

I knew enough to know I was in a battle. But my soul seemed to be ganging up on me. The Holy Spirit was bringing to the light something He wanted me to deal with, and I was tempted to hide. But what He brings to the light, He wants to heal, mend or deliver. The light is a safe place. So, I stayed in the prayer meeting regardless of the desire to run. On the ride home with my husband and kids in the car, I knew I needed a battle plan.

My emotions were screaming at me; "Just leave, go get drunk, you're too responsible, just commit adultery, leave this place. Everyone in your family does that anyway ..."

On and on it went, an endless loop. It had been quite some time since I experienced anything to this magnitude.

We arrived home, and I took my internal war into the house and first went to my room to put on my pajamas. I so badly wanted to run away; I needed that layer of safety. I calmly got my children ready for bed, tucked them in, and prayed under my breath that God would help me not to do anything stupid for their sake. My husband soon retired. I was sitting in the living room alone with war on the inside. The conflict between the spirit and the flesh was real. I wanted to do what was right, but I was also done.

I remember this volcanic urge to bolt began to surface. I immediately hit my face, wrapped my arm around the leg of a chair, and began to pray in tongues. It wasn't but a moment when the Holy Spirit began to groan through me. I had no words, but the Spirit was praying. He was helping me in my weakness—when I did not know how to pray as I should. I wept, and He prayed and groaned through me, interceding for me. How humbling that God would pray for us to make it past our flesh and battles of temptations. I emerged from that prayer rescue, a changed woman. The screaming voice and intense pressure left. It lifted, and I lingered in the presence of God as I became aware I had gotten past a generational stronghold.

4. TONGUES FOR PERSONAL EDIFICATION

I have devoted this entire book to this particular diversity. I challenge you to begin to pray in tongues. Turn the Holy Ghost loose. See if what I am saying is accurate. You will never know unless you try it. I encourage you to share this with someone. Aren't you the least bit curious? I dare you to pray in tongues on purpose and live your life like praying in tongues is normal—because it is!

Pray on saints.

HOW TO PRAY AN HOUR A DAY

I have often been asked, "How did you pray for an hour a day?"

My first answer was, "I was desperate, so I disciplined myself to just do it." I realize that not everyone may be able to do that, so I encourage people to start where they are.

An easy way is to break your hour up. Spend the first 20 minutes in praise and worship, the second 20 minutes praying in the Spirit, and the last 20 minutes confessing the promises of the Word of God. As you grow in your prayer life, you'll find you will have the ability to pray for an hour in tongues. Start where you are. Remember, the devil's strategy is to discourage or condemn you about your prayer life. Just remember, your prayer life is greater than his.

STUDIES ON SPEAKING IN TONGUES

In the book, I promised to talk more about some secular studies that have been done on speaking in tongues (glossolalia). It is fascinating that even secular studies confirm some of the biblical teachings on speaking in tongues. These studies prove the biblical witness of this spiritual gift to be true. In the past, many believed the occurrence to only be an outburst of ecstatic speech. In other words, the speaker had no control. But current studies are proving that speaking in tongues is more of a conscious action and can also help reduce stress.

As mentioned, when one speaks in tongues for edification, the person prays in tongues at will. It is a choice and in their control to do so. While the person may not always have direct control over syllables, they may alter the volume, pitch, and pronunciation. In addition, speaking in tongues has proven to have biological outcomes, such as reduction in stress, which can be summarized as follows:

> "Lynn's team found that glossolalia was associated with both a reduction in circulatory cortisol, and enhancements in alpha-amylase enzyme activity—two common biomarkers of stress reduction that can be measured in saliva. Cortisol is a stress hormone responsible for the familiar stress response known as the fight-or-flight reaction. Alpha-amylase is an arousal enzyme that is sensitive to quick environmental changes and involves adrenaline release in the sympathetic nervous system."[1]

Now, this may simply be the biological explanation, but we know the supernatural explanation. The Holy Spirit, the Comforter, prays through us and releases the peace of God, which surpasses all understanding as we pray.

> "In 2006, a study by researchers at the University of Pennsylvania revealed that after studying brain scans of 5 women praying in tongues that 'their frontal lobes—the thinking, willful part of the brain through which people control what they do—were relatively quiet, as were the language centers. The regions involved in maintaining self-consciousness were active.'"[2]

According to one of the authors of the study, it seemed to confirm that something supernatural was occurring while the participants were speaking in tongues. An article published in *The New York Times* also noted an additional study in England that showed that people who engaged in speaking in tongues rarely had mental problems and were shown to be more emotionally stable than those who did not speak in tongues.[3]

These studies are interesting and helpful, but the greatest way to see if praying in tongues is real is to employ this precious gift in our personal lives.

When I was in school, I wrote a paper on the history of praying in tongues for a college English class. I wish I still had it. I received an "A" regardless of my teacher telling me she thought it was an unusual and difficult subject.

From my study, I recall the first known outpouring in America happened at a school in Topeka, Kansas, in 1901. The minister/teacher was Charles Parham. He was seeking the baptism of the Holy Ghost, as he saw it in the Bible, and was not content to live without it. He, along with several others, wanted an understanding of this gift.

A woman named Agnes Ozman was the first to receive the baptism there and speak in tongues. She spoke in tongues for days. She spoke in a Chinese dialect. She was asked if she could write it, and she did![4]

Soon after, people started being baptized in the Holy Spirit with the evidence of speaking in tongues throughout America. One famous outpouring happened in California with Smith Wigglesworth at the Azusa Street Revival. Many who received the baptism of the Spirit also received their calling to go and preach in other nations. I believe we will see the Holy Spirit poured out upon us once again. He comes in power and demonstration.

I encourage you, once again, be filled with the Spirit and let Him pray through you, for you, and in you. Stay hungry for God.

ENDNOTES

1. Hanson, Dirk. "Speaking in Tongues: Glossolalia and Stress Reduction." Dana Foundation, 17 Aug. 2019, https://dana.org/article/speaking-in-tongues-glossolalia-and-stress-reduction/.

2. Carey, Benedict. "A Neuroscientific Look at Speaking in Tongues." *The New York Times*, The New York Times, 7 Nov. 2006, https://www.nytimes.com/2006/11/07/health/07brain.html.

3. Ibid.

4. This is according to Vinson Synay, Ph.D., taken from the O.R.U. webpage, *The Origins of the Pentecostal Movement*. Dr. Synay teaches Pentecostal History at Oral Roberts University. This was documented at the time by the U.S. government. When language specialists arrived in Topeka, 20 different languages were recorded.

RECOMMENDED RESOURCES FOR FURTHER STUDY

The Walk Of The Spirit—The Walk Of Power
By Dave Roberson
Free Download available on website daveroberson.org

Effective Fervent Prayer
By Mary Alice Islieb

Hidden In Plain View: Unlocking The Mysteries of Tongues.
By Robert Engelhardt

The God I Never Knew
By Robert Morris

The Gifts and Ministries of the Holy Spirit
By Lester Sumrall

Tongues of Fire Devotional: 50 Days Celebrating Pentecost
Whitaker House

Praying In The Holy Spirit
By David Diga Hernandez

Pray In The Spirit
Arthur Walls

Unleashing the Power of Praying in the Spirit
By Oral Roberts

Praying Through: Hidden Truths to Receiving
By Susan Janos and Sara Steele

Tongues
By Kenneth E. Having

Why Tongues
By Kenneth E. Having

Tongues: Beyond the Upper Room
By Kenneth E. Hagen

Baptism in the Holy Spirit
By Kenneth E. Hagen

The Spirit Within and the Spirit Upon
By Kenneth E. Hagen

The Holy Spirit and His Gifts Study Course
By Kenneth E. Hagen

The Expediency of Tongues: The 50 Benefits of Speaking In Tongues (Baptism of the Holy Ghost)
By Plus Joseph

Speaking in Tongues: The Gateway to the Supernatural
By Albert Elisha Oberdorfer

Praying in the Spirit: What it is? Who can do it? How do we do it?
By Terry Ivy

ABOUT THE AUTHOR

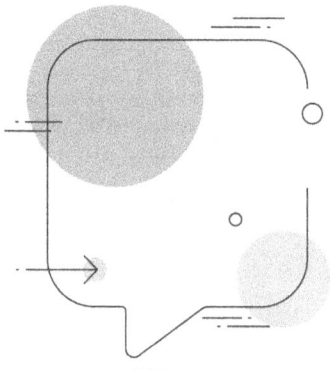

Teresa Verdecchio has a burden for people to experience the joy of being fully known and fully loved by God without shame, fear, or condemnation. She is a wife, mother, grandmother, mentor, author, and teacher. Pastor Teresa has co-labored with her husband, Dave, for over 30 years in ministry, reaching the hearts of men and women domestically and abroad. Together, they are committed to bringing hope to the hopeless, ministering the love of Christ through sound teaching, and tangibly expressing genuine compassion to see broken lives restored.

To learn more or to invite Pastor Teresa to speak at your conference or event:

TERESAVERDECCHIO.COM

DO YOU EVER FEEL LIKE YOU ARE NOT ENOUGH?

Condemnation leaves us spiritually dwarfed and defeated. Voices that make us feel ashamed and unworthy push us to perform to earn God's love and favor. We find it easier to work for God than to be in awe of who He is and wonder about who we are in Him. Traumatic events and hurtful words spoken over us create damage that inflicts pain and hinders joy long after the specific incident is behind us. These wounds can create a vicious cycle of condemnation resulting in self-loathing and unhealthy coping mechanisms that leave you spiritually dwarfed and defeated. Deliverance takes but a moment, but healing is a process. Changing the soundtrack in your mind and living victoriously requires rewiring familiar thought patterns and using spiritual weapons to combat the enemy's offense against your soul. Pastor Teresa Verdecchio candidly shares her story of abuse that became a mindset of condemnation. She walks you through the messy process of healing and deliverance through God's love, and she gives practical tools and strategies to combat condemnation and live in freedom.

BOOK AND STUDY GUIDE AVAILABLE ON **amazon.com**

ACCESS THE AUTHORITY OF THE NAME, THE BLOOD, AND THE CROSS OF CHRIST

What comes from our mouth activates our mind and spirit. When we speak forth the Word of God and come into agreement, we echo God's authority in our life. When we make declarations by faith, we step into dominion through the Name, the Word, The Blood, and the Cross of Christ. Every bondage can be broken. Every wound can be healed. As you journey to freedom, you can access the finished work of Christ and stand in victory.

AVAILABLE ON **amazon.com**

www.ingramcontent.com/pod-product-compliance
Lightning Source LLC
Chambersburg PA
CBHW060353110426
42743CB00036B/2876